"Examine yourselves, to see whether you are in the faith. Test yourselves."

2 Corinthians 13:5

I've Prayed the Prayer

Exposing the Lie of Salvation Without Transformation

Jon Ellis

I've Prayed the Prayer.
Exposing the Lie of Salvation Without Transformation
Published by Uncommon Christian Publishing
PO Box 744
Tallapoosa, Georgia 30176

ISBN:979-8-9985215-0-8

Published in the United States by The Uncommon Christian Publishing

2025--First Edition

Photography and video by Cloud Vue Solutions are used with permission. For more information, visit cloudvuesolutions.com.

To my grandparents, Everett and Beatrice Ellis...

Proof that the prayers of the righteous endure beyond the grave. Thank you for living a faith worth inheriting.

Jon

To my Refuge Ministries staff and family...

Every day, I thank God for the privilege of standing shoulder to shoulder with you in the gospel. This journey has been nothing short of extraordinary. I pray we continue to walk in step with the Holy Spirit, advancing His Kingdom with boldness and unity.

A Personal Word Before You Begin

Before you read a single word...

Let me tell you why I wrote this book.

I've spent years pastoring people who love Jesus, serve faithfully, and possess genuine spiritual hunger—but still quietly question whether they are truly saved. Not because they lack belief, but because, deep down, something has never been transformed.

I've seen it too many times. People walk away from altar calls filled with emotion, but still feel empty inside. Individuals who have prayed the sinner's prayer countless times yet have never experienced peace, freedom, or transformation.

I'm not writing this as a critic; I'm writing as someone who has wept over how far we've drifted from what Jesus actually taught. I'm speaking as a pastor who has sat across from addicts, inmates, husbands, wives, sons, and daughters— whose lives don't reflect the faith they were told to believe in.

I'm writing because I had to confront it myself: what's common in church culture isn't always biblical. And I'm writing because I believe we are living in a generation that's ready—ready to exchange religious clichés for genuine faith, sincere repentance, and true power.

Let me say this clearly...

Dear reader,

This book may challenge you. It might even offend you. Not because I'm trying to stir controversy, but because so much controversy has been generated by many people surrounding one of the most important questions anyone can ask: "What does it actually mean to be 'saved'?"

Regrettably, much of what we encounter in today's church culture does not align with the teachings of Jesus.

We've all heard the phrases:
"Just pray this prayer."
"Once saved, always saved."
"Don't doubt your salvation."

But what if some of the things we've always been told are wrong? I didn't write this to frighten you. I wrote it because I love you too much to stay silent. Eternity is real. Hell is real. And Jesus—King of Kings, Judge of All, Lover of your Soul—said some of the most sobering words in the Bible:

"I never knew you."

And here is what should stop us in our tracks: He wasn't talking to atheists. He was talking to the religious—people who said the right things but never truly surrendered.

I'm not here to argue; I'm here to share the Word, expose the lie, and guide you back to the truth.

And I want to make something clear: this book isn't about fear. If it shakes you, allow it. If it challenges you, embrace it. Because sometimes, God has to shake us to awaken us and refine us to restore us.

Here's my one request:
Continue reading.

Everything comes together in the final chapters. That's where clarity prevails. That's where truth resonates. That's where the next step becomes perfectly clear.

I'm not asking this as an author; I'm asking as a friend, a pastor, and a fellow follower of Jesus. Don't stop when it gets uncomfortable. Don't retreat when it hits too close. Let it finish what it started. Read it all. Complete the journey. Truth is rarely easy, but it's always worth it.

Jon Ellis

CONTENTS

Many were sold a prayer and told it was salvation. But salvation was never a prayer. It was always a Person—Jesus

Introduction

The Moment We've All Experienced

The music swelled in the room, and voices rose as hands lifted. You could feel God's presence settling in the sanctuary. Every song pointed to Jesus, His mercy, grace, and power to save. The musicians played with passion, the choir harmonized like heaven, and something inside you whispered, "God is here."

It was one of those moments when time seemed to freeze. Every lyric hit a little deeper, and the air was thick with something holy. The atmosphere in the room was electric and charged with expectations. The Holy Spirit was at work—there was no doubt about it.

The preacher stepped onto the platform, stood with conviction, and delivered a message of hope and mercy. He proclaimed that no sin is too great for God's forgiveness, that Jesus' grace runs deeper than our deepest failures, and that the cross covers it all. The congregation was locked in, totally captivated. "Whosoever calls on the name of the Lord will be saved!" he declared, and a wave of "Amens!" rolled through the room like thunder. You could feel it—hope rising in the room, quiet and powerful—as the gospel did what only it can do: awaken the heart.

The worship team quietly returned to the stage as the lights dimmed. They played softly underneath the preacher's final words, and the singers began to sing, "Just as I am without one plea." The emotional weight was almost tangible, pressing down on everyone present. Even newcomers sensed the gravity of what was unfolding. Then came the command from the preacher, and it was the moment we'd all experienced.

"Every head bowed, and every eye closed."

A profound silence settled over the congregation—a sacred hush. People shifted nervously in their seats; some gripped the pew in front of them while others bowed their heads instinctively, their bodies familiar with the routine. It felt holy, the kind of moment that grabs your soul and doesn't let go. And then, in a compassionate but firm voice, the pastor issued the familiar invitation many of us have heard our entire lives: "If you want to give your heart to Jesus today, just repeat this prayer after me..." And there it was.

The sinner's prayer.

Heads bowed, eyes closed, words spoken. Tears streamed, hands were raised, and whispers filled the room. When the prayer was finished, the pastor's tone shifted. He no longer spoke softly and invitingly; his voice had become loud and energized. "Praise God!" He exclaimed that new names were being written in the Lamb's Book of Life. "If you just prayed that prayer, welcome to the family of God—you are *saved, sealed, and secure!*" Shouts rang out. Applause filled the sanctuary. The congregation erupted with joy.

As people began to leave the service, they all talked about how powerful, Spirit-filled, and life-changing it was. I don't doubt that some hearts were genuinely transformed that day. Yet, amid all the emotion, celebration, and affirmation, something deeply troubling crept into the church. Despite how powerful the moment felt… we have to ask:

Is this actually what Scripture teaches?

The Question That Changed It All

It happened in the middle of our Sunday night Bible study. A man sitting in the back raised his hand. His voice trembled with frustration. "Pastor Jon, I've been saved multiple times. I've prayed the prayer more times than I can count, but I always seem to go back to the same sins. I do well for a little while, but I end up falling into the same stuff. I don't get it. My past haunts me. I've prayed the sinner's prayer; I've done what they said to do. *So why haven't things changed?*"

The room froze. You could've heard a pin drop. Every eye turned toward me. The weight of his words hit the room like a freight train. I took a deep breath and gently said, "Brother, I hear you. And you're not alone. What I have to say might be hard to hear, but I have to be honest with you— *There is no sinner's prayer in the Bible.*"

That's as far as I got. When I told him there was no sinner's prayer in the Bible, he leaned forward with fire in his eyes and said, "Yes, there is, I've read it, and I've prayed it!

Every pastor I've ever had told me it's in the Bible!"

I responded calmly, "Okay, let's take a look. I've never seen it, but if you have, show me where it is." He flipped frantically through his Bible—pages turning, fingers trembling, mumbling to himself. Occasionally, he would glance up to see if I was still watching. I continued to let him search. His confidence began to unravel.

The Bible study ended, but the weight of that moment lingered. Some left the service with questions, while others departed with conviction. A few appeared confused and concerned. He stayed behind. After everyone had exited, he approached me. He wasn't angry; he was broken.

"Pastor Jon," he said, "I don't understand. I've prayed that prayer so many times. Even on days I didn't feel guilty about anything. I just thought if I said it enough, it would eventually work. I did what they said. I believed in Jesus. I said I was sorry. I told Jesus I wanted to go to heaven. Isn't that enough?"

I wish I could say that moment was rare.

But it's not—it's all too familiar, and that's the problem.

The Man They Called Crazy Horse

People in our town knew the man who asked that question that night as "Crazy Horse." That's not a nickname you give yourself; it gets handed down through stories. And trust me, he has many stories. His reputation involved fighting, drugs, alcohol, and chaos. His past was infamous. People didn't just talk about Crazy Horse; they told legends about him.

That night, when he stood to speak, my 5'7" self looked up at what felt like 8 feet of intensity. My mind raced with the stories I had heard. For a moment, I felt intimidated, but I could see something behind his eyes. There was confusion, desperation, and maybe even hope. That man is the reason I wrote this book. And I am excited to say today that Crazy Horse died. Not physically, but spiritually.

In his place stands Johnny Wayne, a new creation—a man filled with the Spirit, on fire for Jesus, and living proof that genuine repentance leads to true transformation. He serves Jesus in ways that still shock people in our town. Nobody saw it coming, and to be honest, many still don't believe it, but when Jesus steps in, He doesn't just forgive... He resurrects.

Here's the scariest part of the story. For years, Johnny Wayne was led to believe that saying a prayer in a moment guaranteed him heaven. He was taught that he didn't need to worry about repentance, surrender, or transformation if he uttered the right words. He thought he was saved—until he realized he'd placed his faith in a formula, not the Savior.

How Many More Like Him?

That moment with Johnny Wayne lit a fire in my Spirit I couldn't shake.

How many others have done the same thing? How many people have walked an aisle, repeated a prayer, felt a surge of emotion, yet walked away unchanged but thoroughly convinced that they were saved? How many were given a spiritual life jacket that can't save them? How many are clinging to a moment that never turned into a relationship?

This book is not an attack on pastors, churches, or evangelists who lead people in prayer. Many are sincere, and I believe God can work through those moments— I've led people in prayer myself. That's not the issue. The issue is clarity. What it means to be a follower of Jesus is rarely explained.

That's where the disconnect lies.

We need to ask:

- When did repeating a prayer become the new standard for salvation?
- When did a prayer replace true repentance?
- Where did this method originate?
- How did the sinner's prayer become the primary method of "salvation" in the Western church?
- And, most importantly, what does the Bible actually say?

Why This Still Matters

This book is about one thing: TRUTH. Not tradition, not feelings, not what we've always done, nor the familiar script we've memorized. Truth.

Eternity is at stake! If we have believed and preached a gospel without repentance and without following Jesus, we have not truly believed or preached the gospel at all. Furthermore, if we have handed people a half-truth disguised as salvation, we are participating in the greatest deception of our time. Jesus exposed this very problem:

"You have heard that it was said... But I say to you..."
(Matthew 5:21-22)

He didn't just call out sin; He dismantled religious tradition. He exposed belief systems dressed in godliness but stripped of truth. He didn't play it safe or bow to popular opinion—He disrupted the status quo and demanded people return to the authority of God's Word.

That's the kind of boldness we need today. Because, let's be honest—we've been fed lies. We've confused a tearful moment with true conversion. We've replaced costly surrender with convenient simplicity. And it's time to wake up.

We've clung to a man-made formula, slapped a 'saved forever' label on it, and called it the Gospel. But Jesus never offered a formula. He offered a cross.

Let's Unlearn the Lies—And Rediscover Jesus

If what you've always believed was wrong, would you want to know?

This book poses challenging questions. We'll explore the origins of the sinner's prayer and delve into Scripture to uncover what Jesus and the apostles truly taught.

We confront easy believism, call out the false comforts of a repentance-free gospel, and illuminate the narrow road that leads to life. More than anything, this book is your invitation.

An invitation to:

- Test your beliefs.
- Unlearn what culture has taught you.
- Build your faith on truth, not tradition.
- Trade cultural Christianity for devoted discipleship.
- Leave behind the half-gospel and follow Jesus for real.

Salvation isn't just about reciting the right words; it's about following the right Person.

It's about surrendering to a King!

Let's leave the sinner's prayer behind and rediscover what Jesus actually said.

Let's get started.

CHAPTER 1

What Have We Actually Heard?

"You have heard that it was said... But I say to you..."
(Matthew 5:21-22)

We're bombarded by talk of God, faith, and salvation—on stages, in songs, and across screens. But just because it's popular doesn't mean it's biblical. Some of what we have heard is true. Some is twisted. And some? It's just tradition with a Christian label. The more I study, the more I realize something doesn't add up. Somewhere between Jesus' words and our traditions, the truth got buried. Some of the most quoted lines in the church today aren't even in the Bible. They're popular, powerful, catchy, and even sound spiritual—**but God never said that.**

Some of those phrases came from good-hearted leaders who were sincerely wrong. But let's get honest. Here's what we need to ask ourselves:

1. Are we preaching God's truth or merely someone's opinion?
2. Have we mistaken repetition for revelation?

For generations, people have been told that salvation comes through a simple prayer: Bow your head, repeat a few words, say, "Amen," and you're saved. Eternity is guaranteed. But what if we've misheard? What if we've been misled? What if the formula we've built our assurance on isn't in the Bible? What if we've placed our confidence in a script Jesus never gave us? It's time to ask the question:

What have we actually heard?

This isn't just a misunderstanding or a theological disagreement—it's dangerous. If we've misunderstood salvation, we've missed the most essential truth. And that's scary because this misunderstanding has eternal consequences. That's one reason Jesus often said, "You have heard it said... But I say to you..." Jesus wasn't rejecting Scripture. He was exposing how it had been twisted. Assumptions, traditions, and half-truths piled up until what they believed no longer aligned with God's words. And let's be real—it's still happening today—**in churches, in sermons, in us.**

So, what have we really heard about salvation? Who told us that salvation comes from repeating a prayer, and where did they get that idea? This method has become global, but that doesn't mean it's biblical. Have you ever opened your Bible to see if it's in there?

Can you find even one time Jesus or the apostles led someone in a "sinner's prayer"? Have we embraced a tradition because it feels safe and never stopped to ask if it's true?

Truth or Tradition
Can You Tell the Difference?

Let me share a conversation I once overheard at our local Jack's restaurant. A man leaned over to his buddy and said, "Well, you know what the Bible says: love the sinner, hate the sin."

I'd read the Bible cover to cover, and I didn't remember that verse. So, I looked it up. It turns out that Augustine said something like it in the 5th century: "With love for mankind and hatred of sins." Gandhi later popularized it with the phrase, "Hate the sin, not the sinner." Is the concept biblical? Absolutely. Jesus loved sinners. He came to rescue us. But the phrase "love the sinner, hate the sin"? **It's not in the Bible.**

The two men I overheard talking in Jack's that day shared what had been passed down to them. Numerous sayings like this are shared every day. People claim these sayings are from the Bible or that God said them, but that's simply not true.

We've repeated phrases that sound spiritual but never came from God. And the more we hear them, the more we believe them. But repetition doesn't equal revelation. Familiar doesn't mean faithful. Here are just a few of the cultural slogans that have snuck into our theology...

"God helps those who help themselves."
Sounds biblical. It's not. That quote comes from Benjamin Franklin, not God. In fact, the Bible warns: "Cursed is the man who trusts in man and makes flesh his strength..." (Jeremiah 17:5). Total reversal.

"Cleanliness is next to godliness."
It sounds holy. It's hygiene, originating from the 1700s, not the Bible.

"Money is the root of all evil."
Close, but not quite. The Bible says, "For the love of money is a root of all kinds of evils." (1 Timothy 6:10). There is a big difference.

"God works in mysterious ways."
It sounds spiritual and is popular. However, it's not found in the Bible; it originated from an 18th-century hymn by William Cowper.

"God won't give you more than you can handle."
Not true. Wrong verse. Wrong promise. That's a misquote from a verse about temptation. Life will give you more than you can handle—so you'll run to the only One who can. (1 Corinthians 10:13)

"When God closes a door, He opens a window."
That's Hallmark, not Scripture. It sounds nice, but it's simply not biblical. In Acts 16:6-7, Paul wanted to preach in certain places, but God made him wait for a purpose.

"We're all God's children."
Sounds inclusive, but it's not biblical. Without Jesus, we are not adopted; we're lost. (John 1:12)

Why does that matter?

Repetition breeds belief. The more we hear something, the more believable it seems. Repetition fosters familiarity, and familiarity creates false confidence. Over time, we stop questioning what we've always heard, even if it's incorrect. False confidence misleads and will eventually unravel—it did for Crazy Horse, and it will for you, too.

This isn't just about correcting theology—it's about eternal destinies. Many people believe they're saved because they prayed a prayer. They cling to a past moment and the words they repeated after a preacher, who told them, "You're saved. Never doubt it." However, salvation isn't about repeating words; it's about a transformed life.

Jesus warns in Matthew:

> *Not everyone who calls out to me, 'Lord!, Lord!'*
> *will enter the Kingdom of Heaven. Only those*
> *who actually do the will of my Father in heaven*
> *will enter... But I will reply, 'I never knew you.*
> *Get away from me, you who break God's laws.'*
> *(Matthew 7:21; 23 NLT)*

Imagine the horror—someone thinking they're saved, only to hear Jesus say, "I never knew you." Why? Because their faith was built on a moment, not a Master. They trusted in a formula over a relationship.

I'll never forget what Crazy Horse said that night in our Bible study: *"I've prayed the sinner's prayer over and over...* but nothing changes. I still fall into the same temptations. I still feel lost." You could see the defeat in his eyes. He wasn't trying to rebel—he was trying to believe. But somewhere along the way, he had been handed a script without a Savior. **He felt emotion. He experienced the moment. However, there was no transformation.**

What About You?

Maybe you've prayed the sinner's prayer at a youth camp or revival service. You may have been sincere and felt something. But perhaps—like Crazy Horse—you've held onto that moment as proof of your salvation, yet your life has stayed unchanged.

Jesus didn't tell the rich young ruler to recite a prayer. Peter didn't say, "Repeat after me" at Pentecost. Paul never used scripted prayers for salvation. The apostles didn't hand out prewritten cards. Their message was clear:

1. **Repent**
2. **Believe**
3. **Follow**.

So, let's be honest:

Is your salvation rooted in Scripture... or tradition?

If someone asked you how to be saved, what would you say to them? Would your answer come from the Bible or from what you've always heard? If your faith relies more on a past moment than on a present relationship with Jesus, it's time to reassess your foundation.

Where Did This Tradition Originate?

Maybe you're feeling unsettled right now, perhaps a little uneasy. I understand—this truth is hard to confront. The sinner's prayer is so ingrained in modern church culture that challenging it almost feels heretical. But there's no need for guesswork. God's Word speaks clearly. And when we open it, we find a faith that challenges the quick-fix version we've been sold. So, before we unpack the Bible's authentic message of salvation, let's wrestle with one crucial question:

If Scripture doesn't mention the sinner's prayer, why has it become the gold standard in contemporary Christianity?

The truth may shock you, but we must confront it.

CHAPTER 2

Missing the Forest for the Trees

"For judgment I came into this world, that those who do not see may see, and those who see may become blind." (John 9:39)

Missing the Bigger Picture

Have you ever stared at an optical illusion, convinced of what you saw, only to realize it was something entirely different? Maybe it was one of those images that transform into something new when you tilt your screen or close one eye. You saw it. You were sure. And then someone pointed out the truth, and suddenly you couldn't unsee it.

Psychologists refer to this phenomenon as the illusory truth effect—the more frequently you see or hear something, the more likely you are to believe it, even if it's not true. The human brain is wired to recognize patterns. So, when a belief is repeated enough, it sounds and feels like truth. It doesn't require evidence, just repetition. That's how people come to believe lies: not because they were convincing, but because they heard them continually.

Now, consider social media. It's the constant background noise of our lives. Scroll after scroll, reel after reel, post after post—all shaping how we think about God, love, purpose, and identity—viral quotes with "Bible-ish" captions. Emotional music. Pretty fonts. And just enough Scripture to sound legit.

How often have you seen and heard these phrases?
>*"God just wants you to be happy."*
>*"Only God can judge me."*
>*"Follow your heart."*

They're catchy. They're comfortable. And they're not biblical. They're lies—cleverly wrapped in Christian packaging. Most of us don't question them because they don't feel or sound wrong. But deception rarely announces itself. It comes subtly and quietly, camouflaged and familiar. And it's not just on social media; it's in our churches, especially regarding salvation.

The Power of Repetition: When Belief is Disguised as "Truth"

For centuries, the world believed the sun revolved around the Earth—not because there was proof, but because everyone said it did. Ptolemy's geocentric model was accepted for nearly 1,400 years. It wasn't until Copernicus and Galileo challenged the norm that views began to shift. Yet, even then, they labeled Galileo a heretic. Why? Because people repeated the error, not the truth.

The same thing happens today. Many Americans believe that the "separation of church and state" is in the Constitution. It's not. That phrase originated from a letter by Thomas Jefferson in 1802—not the founding documents. However, it's accepted as law because it has been echoed in courtrooms, classrooms, and political debates. That illustrates the power of repetition.

Repetition creates credibility. Not truth.

Even minor biblical misunderstandings prove this:

- Why were we taught that there were three wise men? The Bible never mentions three wise men; it only states that they brought three gifts.

- Why is Satan depicted as a red figure with a pitchfork who rules hell? Satan doesn't rule hell. Revelation 20:10 says he's punished there, not in charge.

If we can be misled about these surface-level details, isn't it possible we've been misled about other things? Things eternal? Like salvation?

The Question Nobody's Asking

Where did the "sinner's prayer" come from — and why did we believe it?

The truth is, it's not in the Bible. Jesus never taught it, and the apostles never used it. Yet, it has been passed down like a sacred tradition. It has been preached, printed, and promoted so widely that many Christians have built their faith on a formula Jesus never gave.

Ask a first-century follower of Jesus how someone is saved, and you would hear words like:
- Repentance and turning away from sin.
- Surrender.
- Death to self.
- Belief in Jesus as King.
- Baptism into His death and resurrection life.

What you wouldn't hear is: **"Repeat this prayer after me."**

Somewhere along the way, the Church began to trade biblical surrender for man-made scripts. What started as a tool to help people respond to Jesus eventually became a replacement for the very relationship it was pointing to.

The Shift: When a Tool Replaced the Truth

In the early Church, following Jesus meant surrendering everything—comfort, safety, even your life. Baptism wasn't a sentimental public announcement or a photo-op; it was a death sentence for your old life. New believers weren't rushed into decisions; they were discipled—sometimes for months—before being baptized. They weren't just prepared for a moment; they were ready for martyrdom.

By the 4th and 5th centuries, the Church aligned with the Roman Empire and evolved into an institution. Power supplanted purity. Ceremonies substituted surrender. Faith became a mere formality. The fire of the Holy Spirit yielded to the structure of religion, replacing the raw, relational call of Jesus to "Follow Me."

The Reformation addressed some of this. Martin Luther and others reminded the Church that salvation is by grace through faith, not by works. However, even they didn't preach the sinner's prayer. They preached: repentance, faith, and transformation.

The modern version of the sinner's prayer emerged centuries later. In the 18th and 19th centuries, **revival came, and so did new methods.**

Revivalists like Charles Finney, Dwight Moody, Billy Sunday, and eventually Billy Graham preached to massive crowds. Televised crusades brought the sinner's prayer into living rooms across America. God used them powerfully. Their motives were sincere; they wanted to help people respond, so they created simple, repeatable methods. However, over time, the sinner's prayer became the message, and we shifted. The prayer became the focus rather than the Person. The moment replaced the movement. The formula became the finish line instead of the starting line.

We've handed down traditions like they're truth. We've made the sinner's prayer the defining moment of salvation—even though the Bible never commands it, models it, or emphasizes it. Somewhere along the line, we traded the call to "repent and follow" for "repeat after me."

And this isn't just theological—it's deeply personal. I'll never forget one night during a powerful community crusade. Over 800 people came forward that week, saying they had accepted Christ. It was one of those undeniable moments when the Holy Spirit was moving, and the atmosphere was charged with conviction.

There was one young man who walked down the aisle that week. He was the son of a very prominent official in our community. The boy stood beside his father, tears in his eyes, and said, "This time, I know it's real." But instead of joy, his father hesitated. He looked at me and said, "He's already been baptized. He's already prayed the prayer. There's no need for all this."

Just like that, the moment passed. The father talked him out of what may have been the first real moment of surrender in his son's life. Why? Years ago, he checked a box. He prayed a prayer, and his father believed that was enough.

This is precisely what happens when we elevate a formula above faith. We strip the gospel of its power by reducing it to a repeat-after-me moment. We miss the Person in favor of the performance. Instead of pointing people to Jesus, we convince them they've already arrived, even though they never started.

When Formula Replaces Faith.

In our microwave culture, formulas are easier than faithfulness. So, we have reduced Christianity to a checklist: go to church, say the prayer, get baptized, post a Scripture—you're in. But Jesus never called us to a formula. He called us to follow. And following costs more than checking boxes. He never gave us a shortcut to holiness; He gave us a cross.

"If any of you wants to be my follower, you must give up your own way, take up your cross daily, and follow me." (Luke 9:23 NLT)

"...count the cost..." (Luke 14:28)

"If you love me, you will keep my commandments." (John 14:15)

Instead of calling people to count the cost, we handed them spiritual prescriptions and coupon codes for heaven. We offered them a prayer instead of the Person of Jesus. No wonder we have churches full of people who prayed the prayer but never changed. They believe in a moment ... but they have never met the Master.

Are We Producing Disciples or Decisions?

*Jesus commanded us in **Matthew 28:19**, "Go therefore and make disciples."*

Making disciples takes time, can be messy, and is something the Church hasn't done. We've traded the process for a moment. We've handed people a script— but not a Savior. We've given them a moment—not a mission. And the result? Confidence in salvation without transformation.

This is dangerous because it gives people a false sense of security while they remain spiritually dead. Saying the words doesn't save you any more than wearing a jersey makes you part of the team. Following Jesus isn't about slogans—it's about surrender. It's not about reciting; it's about repenting. It's not about a one-time decision but a lifetime direction. It's not a formula; it's a faith that follows. And unless we reclaim this truth, we'll keep producing Christians in name only—people who prayed a prayer but never met the Person who saved them.

Our Culture Loves Shortcuts — But God Doesn't Use Them.

We live in a culture that craves convenience. Why meal prep when you can DoorDash? Why study when AI summarizes everything in seconds? Why build character when branding yourself online yields quicker results? Millennials and Gen Z live in the age of shortcuts — life hacks, biohacks, time hacks, even faith hacks. However, shortcuts in the kingdom never lead to transformation. Spiritual transformation doesn't come through shortcuts; it comes through the cross.

There are no hacks for holiness.

The Other Lies We've Repeated

Let's highlight some of the other trees we've been staring at:

"God wants you to be rich." That's not the gospel. That's prosperity distortion. Jesus didn't die so you could upgrade your lifestyle. He died to raise you to a new life.

"Follow your heart." Scripture says, *"The heart is deceitful above all things..."* (Jer. 17:9). We wouldn't follow a known liar; so why follow a deceitful heart?

"Church is optional." Hebrews 10:25 teaches, "Don't neglect gathering together." Streaming sermons in pajamas is not the same as being part of the Body.

"Only leaders are called to ministry." Ephesians 4 teaches that every believer is called and equipped.

These lies became popular not because they were true, but because they were repeated more often than tested. Now, we have TikTok theologians discipling a generation who can quote reels—but cannot recognize the Holy Spirit.

A Story That Hits Home

I've heard stories of men and women who grew up in church, prayed the prayer at age 8, got baptized at 10, but by 16, were living wild. No fruit. No hunger for God. No conviction. Later in life, someone called them to repent, surrender, die to themselves, and follow Jesus. Not to repeat a prayer.

That's when everything changed. The difference wasn't in the words they said; it was in the life they surrendered. **None of them needed a better prayer; they needed a new life.**

Are You Willing to See the Truth?

Maybe you're reading this and thinking, "But I prayed the sinner's prayer. Does that mean I'm not saved?" Let's be clear: a prayer does not save you; Jesus does.

If you've truly believed in Jesus, repented of your sins, and surrendered your life to Him, then you are saved by grace through faith. However, if your confidence lies in the words you repeated rather than the life you surrendered, it's time to reassess where your faith really stands. The test is simple: ask yourself, has my life truly changed? If nothing has changed, then salvation never occurred.

Jesus said in Matthew 7:13-14:

> *"Enter by the narrow gate. For the gate is wide and the way is easy that leads to destruction, and those who enter by it are many. For the gate is narrow and the way is hard that leads to life, and those who find it are few."*

Though well-intentioned, could the sinner's prayer have become the wide gate?

Could it be that in our attempt to make salvation easier, we have widened the gate that Jesus made narrow? Have we cleared the path that was meant to be costly?

Once you see the truth... you can't unsee it. And when you finally see it clearly, it will either set you free — or shatter everything you thought was true about your faith.

If your faith in Jesus hasn't changed your life, you didn't meet Jesus—you made a deal with your guilt.

CHAPTER 3

Easy Believism

The Half-Gospel That's Left Us Empty

"Not everyone who says to me, 'Lord, Lord,' will enter the kingdom of heaven, but the one who does the will of my Father who is in heaven."
(Matthew 7:21)

The Knockoff Gospel

Picture this: It's late. You're scrolling on your phone when you stumble across a deal too good to be true—a brand-new phone that looks exactly like the newest model. It has a sleek design, the right logo, and a price tag that's half the cost. The reviews look solid. The packaging is perfect. The specs are legit. Everything about it screams, "Real deal."

So, you buy it.

At first, it works fine. It looks authentic. Everything seems on point—until it doesn't. A few weeks later, things start glitching. Apps begin crashing. The battery drains within minutes. The operating system won't update. Why? Because it wasn't the real thing. It appeared like the real thing, but it wasn't. You didn't buy the latest model; you bought a knockoff.

And suddenly, the deal no longer feels so sweet. You feel duped. Now you're frustrated. Disappointed. You trusted that phone. You built your life around it—your calendar, communication, photos, and memories—all tied to something that seemed real but failed when it mattered most.

Now imagine that same scenario, not with a phone, but with your soul.

That's what easy believism does. It's a spiritual scam that markets a counterfeit version of Christianity—a half-gospel that promises peace without surrender, grace without repentance, and heaven without a cross. It's spiritual branding, catchy phrases, buzzwords, and emotional hype. And it seems to work for a while until it doesn't. Until sin must be confronted. Until obedience actually costs you something.

That's when it collapses. A fake phone is inconvenient. A fake faith is eternal.

Jesus isn't inviting you to join a trend; He's calling you to transformation. Anything less than that is a knockoff gospel, regardless of how appealing it seems or sounds.

What Is Easy Believism?

Easy believism is the dangerously popular idea that simply believing in Jesus—without repentance, obedience, or discipleship—is sufficient to guarantee salvation. It promotes a hollow gospel: polished, popular, and powerless. Sometimes, it appears as an intellectual agreement: believe in Jesus, check the box, and move on.

Other times, it manifests as an emotional experience: a quick prayer, a few tears, a walk down the aisle, a spiritual buzz, followed by continuing to live the same way. It asserts, "As long as you believe in Jesus, you're saved." No surrender. No repentance. No obedience. No discipleship. No dying to self. Just believe.

You've heard the slogans before:

> **"Jesus loves you just as you are."**
> **"Once saved, always saved... no matter what."**
> **"Just believe and receive."**

They sound nice—comfortable and safe—but they're not biblical. Here's the truth: belief alone isn't saving faith. Even James called that out.

"You believe that there is one God. Good! Even the demons believe that— and shudder." (James 2:19 NIV)

Demons believe in Jesus. They don't question His lordship, nor do they deny His power. They know exactly who He is—and they tremble. So, here are the uncomfortable questions:

- **If our belief does not lead to transformation, what distinguishes it from theirs?**
- **Do we possess the same type of faith as demons?**

It's easy to say no, but let's dig deeper.

Do we:
- Believe in Jesus yet refuse to obey Him?
- Acknowledge His name, but live our own way?
- Claim salvation but reject surrender?

James didn't stop at mere belief; he went further by stating: *"...faith apart from works is dead." (James 2:26)*

Not because works save us, but because true faith can't remain buried; it's alive. True faith obeys, repents, and produces fruit. A faith that never results in transformation isn't saving faith—it's a lie dressed in Christian language.

What Easy Believism Gets Wrong

When someone truly encounters Jesus, they don't merely admire Him; they follow Him. They don't just agree with Him; they build their lives around Him.

Easy believism strips the Gospel of its power. It offers a crown without a cross, comfort without conviction, a Savior without Lordship, and heaven without holiness. Jesus never preached that gospel.

"If anyone would come after Me, let him deny himself and take up his cross daily and follow me."
(Luke 9:23)

That's not easy. It's death to self. It means losing your life so you can find it. That's transformation. Here's the danger: easy believism convinces people they're safe when they've never truly surrendered. It doesn't just confuse people; it condemns them. It tells people they're born again even when they've never truly died.

How Did We Get Here?

Jesus called people to die to themselves. So, how did we end up with a gospel that says, "Just believe and you're in"? The shift was subtle. We shifted from discipleship to decisions. From "Come and die" to "Come and decide." From transformation to a transaction. Jesus never said, "Raise your hand and repeat after Me." He said:

"If anyone would come after me, let him deny himself and take up his cross, and follow me."
(Matthew 16:24)

His mission wasn't to make converts; it was to make disciples. While men like Charles Finney, Billy Sunday, and Billy Graham preached the gospel passionately, with urgency and sincerity, their genuine desire to reach souls was powerful, and God used them mightily. However, something shifted: evangelism became a moment rather than a movement. The starting line became the finish line.

In trying to make the Gospel more accessible, the Church unintentionally made it more shallow. In its efforts to reach further, the church began measuring success by the number of decisions made, not the number of disciples formed. Why? Because decisions are easier to count. Discipleship takes time. It requires walking with people through conviction, repentance, accountability, and submission to the Holy Spirit. However, when you reduce salvation to a decision instead of a new direction, you create a generation of churchgoers who believe they're saved because of something they said, even if nothing about their lives ever changed.

Too many have come to Jesus not because of who He is, but because they're trying to avoid where they're going. They didn't fall in love with the Savior—they just wanted fire insurance. But escaping hell isn't the same as surrendering to Jesus. Salvation should never be a fear-based transaction, but a love-driven surrender. If your decision to follow Him wasn't rooted in repentance and a desire to know Him, you didn't meet Jesus—you just made a deal with your own guilt.

The Fruit of Easy Believism

When salvation turns into a one-time prayer, the result is false converts—people who experience a moment but are never truly made new. They may have cried. They may have felt something. They may have even gotten baptized. But they were never born again. And you can see the fruit—or the lack of it everywhere.

- Churches filled with people living in open sin.
- Christians lacking a desire for holiness.
- Believers are unaffected by the Word.
- Hearts remain unmoved by conviction.

Why has this happened? Because somewhere along the way, they were told, "If you prayed that prayer, you're good." But Jesus never said, "You'll know them by their confession." He said: *"You will recognize them by their fruits." (Matthew 7:16)*

In Matthew 13, Jesus presented a Parable of the Soils—not as a farming lesson, but as a heart check. Let's break it down:

Jesus described four types of soil:

1. **The Pathway:** A hard surface where the seed never sinks in. The Word is heard but quickly stolen. There is no openness. No roots. Just rejection.

2. **The Rocky Ground:** Emotional excitement arises. A spiritual buzz. Yet, there is no root, no depth, no foundation. Trials come, and it dies.

3. **The Thorny Soil:** Growth begins, but worry, greed, busyness, and distractions choke it out.

4. **The Good Soil:** The heart receives the Word, digs deeply, and bears fruit over time.

Some hear but never truly receive. Some get excited but eventually fall away. Some start strong but get choked out by distractions. Only one type of soil produces lasting fruit—the one that doesn't just hear the Word, but receives it, roots itself in it, and is transformed by it. That's the mark of true salvation.

The soil reveals the root.
The fruit reveals the truth.

This is where the modern church must wake up. Genuine faith bears real fruit:

- Repentance
- Obedience
- Holiness
- Perseverance
- A growing hunger for Jesus.

If these are missing, it doesn't matter what prayer you prayed or how many times you've been baptized. Jesus said, "You will know them by their fruit."

What Jesus Said About Salvation

Let's strip away the slogans. Forget the formulas and return to the source. What did Jesus say about salvation? His words weren't soft. They weren't vague. They were clear and direct:

- *"Repent and believe the gospel." (Mark 1:15)*
- *"Take up your cross and follow me." (Luke 9:23)*
- *"Whoever loses his life for my sake will find it." (Matthew 10:39)*

Notice what's not in there:
- "Repeat after me."
- "Invite me into your heart."
- "Check the box."

Do you see the difference? Jesus didn't offer comfort; He offered crosses. He didn't ask for recited prayers; He called for surrendered lives. Yes, salvation is by grace, but that grace isn't cheap. It cost Jesus His life, and it will cost you your old one.

If your faith in Jesus has not changed your old life or transformed your heart, you have fallen for the lie of easy believism.

Modern-Day Knockoffs

You don't have to look far to see easy believism; we see it everywhere.

- **The Prosperity Gospel** preaches breakthroughs, blessings, and abundance, while omitting mentions of sin, repentance, sacrifice, or surrender. In that gospel, Jesus serves as a life coach rather than a Lord.

- **Cultural Christianity** views being a "Christian" as a label rather than a way of life. It emerges during Easter and Christmas, quotes a few verses, and lives like everyone else. No repentance. No relationship. No pursuit of holiness.

- **Hyper-Grace Theology** dismisses obedience as legalism and views repentance as optional. It weaponizes grace to suppress conviction and justify sin.

These all have different flavors but share the same fatal flaw: salvation without surrender, a Savior without lordship, and faith without fruit. They preach Jesus as a mascot, not a Master. They may start with truth—but they end in error. They promise fullness, but leave you empty. They offer salvation but deliver deception.

Final Challenge: Have You Truly Surrendered?

Let's be real—this chapter may feel like a gut punch. That's okay; it's not meant to scare you. It's here to awaken you.

So let me ask you:
- Have you truly surrendered your life to Jesus?
- Was your salvation an event in the past or a transformation?
- Is your faith rooted in a moment, or in a Master?
- Have you followed Jesus, or simply agreed with Him?

This book isn't trying to make you doubt—it's helping you discern. Jesus isn't calling you to a moment of surrender; He's calling you to a life of surrender. And here's the good news: If you've been chasing a knockoff gospel, it's not too late to trade it in for the real thing. You don't need to fake it. You don't need to wonder. You can follow Jesus fully today.

Belief was never meant to be the end.
It was always supposed to be the beginning—
of surrender, of transformation,
of true life in Jesus.

CHAPTER 4

The Half-Built Bridge

Why the Gospel Without Repentance Fails

"No, I tell you; but unless you repent,
you will all likewise perish."
(Luke 13:3)

The Half-Built Bridge: A Dangerous Shortcut

My wife and I have been together since we were 14 years old. Over the years, God has truly blessed us with the opportunity to travel a lot. From the North Georgia mountains to the beaches of Cape Town, South Africa, Israel, and the Mediterranean, we've seen some beautiful places together. But here's the thing: we travel very differently.

We are rarely on the same page when it comes to traveling. Get my wife to a beach, and she's already got her feet in the sand before I can unload the SUV. Drop her in the mountains, and she's off exploring and shopping like she owns the place. And roller coasters?

Don't even get me started. She's fearless, sitting in the front row with her hands up, laughing like a maniac, while I'm gripping the harness and praying in some kind of tongue to survive the ride.

I'm just wired differently. I overthink everything. I want to know who built the ride, when it was last inspected, and whether the architect double-checked the math. This is especially true when I step onto those long suspension bridges in a park that look safe but make my stomach flip. That's when I start questioning everything. Did they test this with real people? Will this thing actually hold?

And just like that, something clicked. This isn't just about a bridge; it's a representation of what millions experience spiritually. They step onto something that appears trustworthy and feels right. It's labeled with grace, forgiveness, and even Jesus. However, somewhere in the middle, a question strikes them: 'Will this actually carry me to the other side?'

That's when the truth starts to surface—the realization that something crucial is missing. This path won't lead them where they thought it would. That's exactly what a repentance-free gospel does. It looks like salvation. It feels like hope. It sounds like the truth. But it lacks the one thing that connects us to new life: **Repentance.**

Without repentance, the gospel resembles a half-built bridge. It offers people enough truth to begin their journey, yet it never encourages them to turn from sin and genuinely follow Christ. However, Jesus didn't construct a halfway bridge. He laid himself down as the sole path across. He didn't create a shortcut; He became the way, the truth, and the life—no one crosses over except through Him.

Millions of churchgoers are currently halfway across this bridge, convinced they're safe because of a prayer they prayed, unaware they've never surrendered, never repented, and never changed. Think about it. Jesus never did anything halfway. And He certainly didn't build a bridge to halfway holiness. He built a narrow road that demands complete surrender. It's the only way to the other side.

What Is Repentance?

The word "repentance" has nearly disappeared from many pulpits. It's often replaced with softer phrases like "invite Jesus into your heart" or "make a decision for Christ." But is that really what Jesus preached? Not even close. Repentance is more than feeling sorry. It's a radical turning—a complete change of mind, heart, and direction. The Greek word *metanoia* means "a change of mind." But it's not just about thought; it's a change that reorients your whole life. Repentance impacts your attitude toward sin, understanding of who Jesus is, and what it means to follow Him. It starts with recognizing your sin and agreeing with God that your way is wrong:

"For I know my transgressions, and my sin is ever before me. Against you, you only, have I sinned and done what is evil in your sight..."
(Psalm 51:3-4)

It requires a conscious choice to abandon a lifestyle of sin:

"Repent therefore, and turn back, that your sins may be blotted out" (Acts 3:19)

And it produces fruit—evidence of transformation.

"Bear fruits in keeping with repentance." (Luke 3:8)

True repentance doesn't merely ask for forgiveness. It leads to transformation. A changed mind leads to a changed life.

Jesus Preached Repentance—Why Don't We?

From the very beginning, Jesus' message was clear and uncompromising:

> *"Repent, for the kingdom of heaven is at hand."*
> *(Matthew 4:17)*

He didn't ease into it. He led with it. In Luke 13:3, He warned:

> *"No, I tell you; but unless you repent, you will*
> *all likewise perish." (Luke 13:3)*

In John 8:11, He looked a woman caught in adultery in the eye and said:

> *"Neither do I condemn you; go, and from now on*
> *sin no more." (John 8:11)*

Jesus never invited anyone to say a prayer. He called them to turn, surrender, and follow Him. So why has the modern Church drifted from preaching repentance? Because it's uncomfortable. It confronts lifestyles. It pushes against culture. And in a world obsessed with self, repentance sounds offensive. It suggests you're not okay the way you are and need to submit to someone greater. **It's not "seeker-friendly."**

Many churches have exchanged the gospel for motivation. They want people to feel inspired, not convicted. They aim to grow crowds, not to convict them. So, they present a Jesus who blesses your plans but never asks you to surrender them. And repentance? It quietly gets overlooked—not entirely denied, just neglected until it fades into the background.

There's another reason: it's easier to count decisions than to make disciples. A packed altar call resembles revival. However, if sin isn't forsaken and lives aren't surrendered, then we're just giving people false assurance. We're celebrating emotion, not transformation.

So, what happens when repentance is removed? You get a gospel that appears hopeful, sounds gracious, and feels truthful—but it's incomplete. It starts strong but doesn't lead to life. Without repentance, we're inviting people onto a half-built bridge. One day, they'll realize it never had the power to carry them across.

The Consequence: False Converts and a Powerless Church

A gospel without repentance produces false converts— people who believe they're saved but whose lives show no evidence of Christ.

No transformation.

No fruit.

No surrender.

Jesus made it painfully clear: not everyone who calls Him "Lord" will enter the Kingdom—but only those who actually do the will of the Father. He warned that many will one day point to their spiritual activity, only to hear Him say they were never truly His.

Let that sink in.

Every person will stand before God. There will be no hiding behind good intentions, church attendance, or emotional altar calls. Can you imagine believing you were saved, only to realize, too late, that you were never born again? That's not a fear tactic. That's a reality for countless people who were told they were fine… but were never told to repent and obey the gospel.

This is the danger of a repentance-free gospel. It creates fans of Jesus, not followers. People claim Jesus as Savior but not as Lord. They desire heaven without holiness, forgiveness without obedience, and a cross that saves but not one to carry. When repentance is removed, the Church loses its power. Sin is no longer confronted; it's tolerated. Holiness is replaced by hype.

Entire denominations have traded truth for cultural acceptance. As a result, churches become filled with people who "made a decision for Christ" but now live in open rebellion—without conviction, correction, or fruit. That's what occurs when we erase the very first word of the gospel—repent. Without it, we're not preaching Christ's message; we're preaching comfort with a Christian label.

When repentance is ignored:
- **The gospel becomes diluted.**
- **Discipleship becomes optional.**
- **The Church becomes powerless.**

We're left with crowds but no commitment, emotion but no obedience, noise but no transformation. Ultimately, we end up with people who believe they're on the narrow road... but have never left the broad one.

Real Salvation Produces Real Change

The true gospel hasn't changed. Scripture never separates faith from repentance; they are two sides of the same coin. Faith turns toward Jesus, while repentance turns away from sin. You can't cling to Christ and your sin simultaneously; one hand must let go.

"I did not shrink from declaring to you anything that was profitable ... testifying both to Jews and to Greeks of repentance toward God and of faith in our Lord Jesus Christ." (Acts 20:20-21)

This is the message that the early Church preached. It's the gospel with the power to save. That's the message we must return to if we want to see lives truly changed and the Church walking in power again.

Salvation isn't just a moment—it's a miracle. It's not about adding Jesus to your life; it's about Jesus transforming your life from the inside out. When someone truly encounters the risen Christ, something shifts. Old desires begin to fade, and new passions come alive. A hunger for holiness replaces the appetite for sin. Genuine salvation produces real change.

That doesn't mean perfection—it means direction. You may stumble, but you don't stay down. You may wrestle, but you no longer make peace with sin. Why? Because the Spirit of God now lives in you. And He refuses to let you remain the same. A gospel that doesn't lead to transformation isn't the gospel of Jesus. It might be popular, polished, or even influential, but it's powerless.

In the end, it will leave people lost. It's one thing to walk halfway across a broken bridge—it's another to lead others there too. That's the weight we carry if we don't return to the gospel Jesus actually preached. Yet, this powerless gospel has taken on many forms—modern counterfeits that parade as truth but lead people further from the cross.

Let's Name the Counterfeits

Today, we have exchanged the true gospel for modern counterfeit versions of Christianity that may sound appealing but require no repentance. Let's name them:

The Self-Help Gospel tells you that you are enough, just as you are. It swaps sin for self-esteem and replaces the cross with cliches. Jesus becomes a motivational speaker, not a risen King. *It builds confidence but not conviction.*

The Church Club Mentality treats Christianity like a social identity instead of a surrendered life. As long as you show up, serve occasionally, and say the right things, you're "in." *Jesus becomes a mascot for morality rather than the Master of your soul.*

The "Come As You Are, Stay As You Are" Gospel celebrates Jesus' love and acceptance but overlooks His call to change. Yes, Jesus meets us in our mess—but He never leaves us there. *It comforts people into complacency rather than calling them to transformation.*

The Deconstruction Movement begins by questioning church hurt, legalism, and hypocrisy, which can be valid, but often concludes by dismantling biblical truth entirely. Jesus becomes an idea to reimagine rather than a Lord to obey. *It persuades people that tearing down the truth is equivalent to finding freedom.*

The result?

Millions of people who believe they're saved but have never repented, surrendered, or followed Jesus.

The Invitation Jesus Actually Gave

Jesus never said, "Accept Me into your heart." He never said, "Repeat this prayer."

He said things like:
> *"Whoever does not bear his own cross and come after me cannot be my disciple."* **(Luke 14:27)**

And:
> *"For whoever would save his life will lose it, but whoever loses his life for my sake will find it."* **(Matthew 16:25)**

This is the true gospel. Not an invitation to convenience but to consecration. Not a message of comfort, but a call to carry the cross. Not just to believe—but to surrender everything.

Final Challenge: Have You Truly Repented?

Let's be honest.

- Have you truly repented... or just become comfortable on the bridge?
- Have you turned from your sin, or did you pray a prayer and keep walking your way?
- Have you confused church attendance, emotional experiences, or Christian language for saving faith?
- Have you made peace with sin instead of making war against it?

Jesus isn't looking for fans; He's calling for followers—not just those raising their hands, but those laying down their lives. True faith is always proven by a transformed life. The grace that saves also changes, and the cross that redeems also requires. It's time to leave behind the half-built bridge. It's time to reject the powerless gospel of comfort and convenience. It's time to return to the message Jesus preached: **Repent. Believe. Follow.** That's the only road that leads to life.

CHAPTER 5

Great Expectations:

What Following Jesus Really Means

"And he said to all, 'If anyone would come after me, let him deny himself and take up his cross daily and follow me.'" (Luke 9:23)

The Reality Check: What Did You Expect?

Imagine signing up for a marathon and being told, "Just show up, put on a number, and you'll get a medal." No mention of the training, the discipline, or the pain ahead—just the promise of reward. So, you start excited, intense, and full of energy—until your legs ache, your lungs burn, and the joy fades into exhaustion.

What was sold as easy turns out to require everything.

That's the bait-and-switch many people experience in the Christian life. They're sold a version of Jesus that offers peace without pressure, purpose without pain, and salvation without surrender. They hear about grace, forgiveness, and heaven, but no one mentions the cross they're expected to carry. So, when life hits hard, they wonder what went wrong.

But the truth is: nothing went wrong. They were just never told what Jesus actually said.

Jesus never baited people with false promises. He never buried the fine print in theological jargon. He didn't recruit fans; He called followers. And He was brutally honest about the cost.

"If anyone would come after me, let him deny himself and take up his cross daily and follow me."
(Luke 9:23)

This wasn't a metaphor—it was a mission.

The invitation was for anyone. But the cost? It's the same for everyone: **die daily**. The Christian life is not just about making a decision. It's about following through to the finish.

The Myth of Cheap Grace

We live in a culture addicted to convenience: fast food, same-day shipping, swipe-right dating, instant gratification, and even AI discipleship. Everything is designed for speed and comfort. Unfortunately, this same mindset has infiltrated many pulpits. Christianity is now marketed like a product: low effort, high reward. Heaven without holiness. Blessing without burden. Cross sold separately.

Grace is repackaged as a one-time transaction instead of a lifelong transformation. "Pray the prayer," they say, "and you're good." But that's not the gospel Jesus preached. That's what Dietrich Bonhoeffer called cheap grace in his book *The Cost of Discipleship*:

"Cheap grace is grace without discipleship, grace without the cross, grace without Jesus Christ, living and incarnate."

Bonhoeffer didn't just write those words—he lived them. While much of the church in Nazi Germany compromised with power, Bonhoeffer chose the narrow road. He trained disciples in secret. He defied Hitler, was arrested, imprisoned, and eventually executed. Why? Because he believed that grace demands obedience and that faith without action isn't faith at all.

Cheap grace says: "Jesus died, so I don't have to change."

Real grace says: "Jesus died so I can be changed— and keep changing."

Cheap grace offers a get-out-of-hell-free card. Real grace gives you a cross. One allows you to remain comfortable in your sin, while the other leads you toward freedom from it.

Francis Chan wrote in his book *Crazy Love*:

"Lukewarm people don't really want to be saved from their sin; they want only to be saved from the penalty of their sin."

That's what happens when we preach grace without transformation.

Today's church is filled with people who believe that God's grace gives them permission to remain unchanged. But grace isn't permission; it's **power**. Power to turn from sin. Power to obey. Power to follow Jesus when it costs you everything.

Grace doesn't lower the bar; it lifts the sinner.

It's as if someone wears a wedding ring but lives as though they're single. No commitment. No intimacy. Just a symbol with no substance. Sadly, that's what many now refer to as Christianity—a symbol without surrender.

But Jesus didn't die to provide us with a symbol; he died to give us new life.

Scripture is clear:

True grace transforms:

"What shall we say then? Are we to continue in sin that grace may abound? By no means!" (Romans 6:1-2)

Faith is proven by action:

"For as the body apart from the spirit is dead, so also faith apart from works is dead." (James 2:26)

Salvation requires endurance:

"But the one who endures to the end will be saved." (Matthew 24:13)

If grace doesn't change you, you haven't truly received it.

We've replaced altars with attendance cards. But Jesus didn't say, "fill a seat." He said, "Take up your cross." He warned of what happens to those who start the race but fail to prepare.

The Ten Virgins–A Warning to the Unprepared

In Matthew 25, Jesus tells a haunting parable. Ten virgins with ten lamps are all waiting for the Bridegroom. On the surface, they all seem ready. However, only five brought extra oil; the other five were unprepared because the Bridegroom was delayed. When the Bridegroom arrived, it was too late. The five foolish ones begged for access and cried out, but the door was shut. Jesus said, "I never knew you."

Let that sink in.

These weren't wild rebels. They weren't mocking God. They were waiting. They were dressed. They held lamps in hand. They looked ready. But they had no reserve. No extra. There had been no preparation.

The lamp represents their profession of faith—the part visible to others. The oil symbolizes their preparation—genuine conversion, intimacy with Jesus, and a lasting connection to the Holy Spirit. This parable dispels the myth that merely starting the race and appearing committed ensures you'll finish it. Jesus concludes the parable with a warning:

"Watch therefore, for you know neither the day nor the hour." (Matthew 25:13)

So why did only five bring extra oil? They didn't just rely on the oil they received at the beginning. They were willing to dig deeper, wait longer, and do whatever it took to store more oil for later. Their preparation after receiving their oil revealed a genuine transformation.

Jesus wasn't expecting perfection—He was expecting preparation. He was looking for those who live ready, stay filled, and depend on Him daily. You can't borrow someone else's oil—and you can't fake a faith that was never truly yours.

The ten virgins serve as a warning to the unprepared—but Judas? Judas is a warning to the unfaithful. Because it's one thing to appear ready on the outside. It's another to choose to betray the One you once walked with.

Judas–A Chosen Apostle Who Walked Away

Judas wasn't on the outside looking in; he didn't just hear about Jesus; he walked with Him. He healed the sick, cast out demons, and preached the kingdom. He was present when Jesus promised that the Twelve would sit on thrones judging Israel (Matthew 19:28). Judas was included in that promise, but he traded it all for 30 pieces of silver.

And here's the sobering truth: he didn't wake up one day and decide to betray Jesus. The drift began small—a touch of greed, a hint of frustration, a bit of compromise. Until one day, it became a kiss—a decision that sealed his fate.

Here's the truth we haven't been told, and most people don't want to hear:

You can be chosen and still fall away. You can walk with Jesus and still reject Him. You can perform miracles and still miss the kingdom.

Judas isn't just an exception. He's a warning.

"If we endure, we will also reign with him; if we deny him, he also will deny us." (2 Timothy 2:12)

"Take care, brothers, lest there be in any of you an evil, unbelieving heart, leading you to fall away from the living God." (Hebrews 3:12)

Salvation isn't sealed by a moment. It's proven over a lifetime.

Salvation Is a Journey: Not Just a Decision

Following Jesus isn't just a one-time prayer followed by a lifetime of passivity. It involves a daily death, a daily choice, and a daily pursuit of the One who gave everything. Notice what Jesus told His disciples when it came to following Him:

"For which of you, desiring to build a tower, does not first sit down and count the cost...?" (Luke 14:28)

If you only lay a foundation and never finish the building, what's the point? It's the same with following Jesus. Faith isn't proven by saying yes in a moment, but by the life you build afterward. It's not about the hype at the start—it's about being faithful to the end.

Cultural Christianity loves a Savior but ignores the Lord. It desires heaven later without pursuing holiness now. However, Jesus cannot be divided. You either follow all of Him, or you follow none of Him.

Why 'Once Saved, Always Saved' Is Dangerous

This teaching has lulled millions into a state of spiritual apathy.

Here's why it's dangerous:

1. **It offers a false sense of security.** It leads people to believe they are safe, even while living in rebellion. There is no holiness, no repentance, and no hunger for God—just a faint recollection of an emotional moment they experienced years ago. Now, they assume their eternity is secure.

2. **It ignores clear biblical warnings.** Scripture doesn't say, "You're good because you started." It says: "The one who endures to the end will be saved." (Matthew 24:13). Jesus warned us about seeds that sprout quickly but have no root, lamps that run out of oil, and branches that don't bear fruit. Over and over, we're told to remain, abide, overcome, and keep the faith. If salvation were simply a one-time decision with no follow-through, why would Jesus and the apostles repeatedly warn believers not to fall away?

3. **It's creating a church that is comfortable, carnal, and asleep.** People call Jesus "Lord," but they don't do what He says. They quote verses but don't live them. They sing about surrender on Sunday and live for themselves the rest of the week. We've raised a generation that treats obedience like an optional add-on. It turns the cross into a comfort zone and grace into a license to drift. That's not salvation. That's deception.

The church's purpose was never meant to be a cruise ship for the comfortable but a lifeboat for the desperate, not a museum of tradition but a movement of transformation.

And yet, here we are—entertained, emotional, and empty.

The church is not healthy because we've sold her a lie. We've told her she can have Jesus without the cross, grace without obedience, and heaven without holiness.

But Jesus never said, "Once you say it, you're set forever."

He said:

> *"Whoever does not bear his own cross and*
> *come after me cannot be my disciple."*
> *(Luke 14:27)*

A memory doesn't prove salvation—it's revealed by a life. If you started the race but quit running, you didn't lose your salvation—you proved you never surrendered. **True salvation finishes. True faith endures.** There is no salvation without surrender. No grace without repentance. No crown without the cross.

The Cost of Following Jesus

Following Jesus will cost you everything.

- **Dying to self:** *"I have been crucified with Christ. It is no longer I who live, but Christ who lives in me." (Galatians 2:20)*

- **Obedience:** *"If you love me, you will keep my commandments." (John 14:15)*

- **Endurance:** *"…let us run with endurance the race that is set before us." Hebrews 12:1*

Paul didn't just preach this; he lived it. Shipwrecked, imprisoned, beaten, persecuted—and eventually martyred. And still, he wrote:

"I have fought the good fight, I have finished the race, I have kept the faith." (2 Timothy 4:7)

Many start the race, but few finish well. Here's the exciting part for those who do:

"Be faithful unto death, and I will give you the crown of life." (Revelation 2:10)

Final Challenge: Are You Truly Following Jesus?

Let's be honest.

- Did you pray a prayer but never truly surrender?
- Are you running the race, or are you standing still?
- If following Jesus cost you everything, would you still follow?

This isn't about checking boxes. This is about dying daily.

Jesus didn't say, "Decide." He said, "Die."

I titled this chapter *"Great Expectations"* because the gospel sets a high standard of holiness, perseverance, and unwavering love. So, ask yourself and base it on everything Scripture says about marriage, purity, repentance, and readiness:

Do you truly believe Jesus is returning for those who aren't prepared, aren't watching, and aren't longing for Him?

John Bevere said it bluntly:

"Do you really think Jesus is coming back after a bunch of half-hearted harlots?"

It may sound intense, but it resonates with the very heart of Jesus. He's not returning for a bride who flirted with Him once and then lived for herself. He's returning for a faithful Church, set apart, burning with love, and fully awake.

The "once saved, always saved" teaching promises security but delivers complacency. It numbs believers into thinking their lives can remain unchanged. However, true salvation doesn't just save us—it transforms us. Jesus never offered false assurance; He instead presented a cross and calls us to carry it daily.

So, here's your moment. Not the emotional one, but the eternal one. The one where you ask yourself:

"Am I truly following Jesus... or just wearing His name?"

When Jesus returns, He won't be searching for borrowed oil, or church attendance records. He's coming for hearts fully surrendered, lamps filled with oil, and lives that bear the marks of the cross. Make sure you're not just in the crowd. Make sure you're truly in Christ.

This isn't a call to try harder. This is a call to die deeper.

CHAPTER 6

Contender or Pretender?

"Examine yourselves, to see whether you are in the faith. Test yourselves. Or do you not realize this about yourselves, that Jesus Christ is in you?— unless indeed you fail to meet the test!"
(2 Corinthians 13:5)

A Startling Realization

He had been in church for 40 years. He led small groups, taught Sunday school, and helped plant a church. He had prayed the prayer, lifted his hands in worship, and learned the language of faith. On the surface, he looked like a pillar of the church.

But one Sunday, in the back row of a quiet sanctuary, something shattered his certainty. The message wasn't new—but this time, it confronted him. A single verse struck like lightning, and in the moment, he saw it clearly: he had believed... but never truly followed. Trusted Him... but never surrendered. His faith had been shallow, his heart untouched. And as conviction crashed in, the truth became unbearable—he wasn't saved. **He had been a pretender.** But now, for the first time, he was ready to become a contender.

What if you spent your whole life believing you were saved, only to stand before Jesus and hear the most devastating words imaginable?

"I never knew you."

That's not just a nightmare; it's a reality Jesus warned us about. And it's not for the atheist, the agnostic, or the openly rebellious. It's for the one who sat in church, read the Bible, served on teams, and still missed it. This chapter is a wake-up call—not for the skeptic, but for the self-assured.

For the one who wears the label "Christian" but has never truly surrendered to Christ. For the one who believes in Jesus but doesn't follow Him. For the one who looks the part yet lives unchanged. It's time to ask the question no one wants to pose: **Am I a contender or a pretender?**

A Fake Diamond: It Shines... Until It Shatters

This image isn't about jewelry. It's about faith. Fake faith, like a fake diamond, sparkles in the spotlight. It catches attention. It looks flawless at first glance. But appearance can't withstand pressure. The true test of a diamond isn't how it shines in peace—it's how it holds up under pressure. And when the pressure comes? Fake faith cracks. Trials expose it. Temptations shatter it. Truth scorches it. It dazzles in daylight but disintegrates in the dark. It may impress the crowd, but it can't stand before Christ.

That's why Jesus didn't just warn about sin—He warned about deception. Not just rebellion, but pretending. Not just failure, but faking it. You can look the part and still not pass the test. Because real faith isn't proven by how loud you shout—it's proven by what survives the fire.

Jesus didn't leave room for ambiguity. During the Sermon on the Mount, He made it clear: On the day of judgment, many will expect to be welcomed into Heaven... only to be turned away.

> *"On that day many will say to me, 'Lord, Lord, did we not prophesy in your name, and cast out demons in your name, and do many mighty works in your name?' And then will I declare to them, 'I never knew you; depart from me, you workers of lawlessness.'" (Matthew 7:22-23)*

That's not a warning for people outside the church; it's for those inside it. These individuals preached, served, and performed miracles. They were active but not surrendered. They appeared impressive in this world, yet remained unknown in heaven. They were pretenders.

The Apostle Paul said that in the last days there would be people *"having the appearance of godliness, but denying its power" (2 Timothy 3:5).* They bore the name of Jesus but lived apart from His Lordship. Jesus won't say, 'Well done, good and faithful attendee.' He's looking for surrendered disciples, not polished pretenders.

The Marks of a Pretender

Pretenders master performance, learn the language, mimic motions, and blend into the community. But here's what can't be staged: a transformed heart.

Jesus called them tares among the wheat—same field, same sun, same rain—but no fruit. No root. Just imitation. And in today's church culture, imitation thrives. We've lowered the bar. We've substituted inspiration for transformation. We've traded surrender for a scripted prayer.

It's tempting to assume Jesus was only speaking about those in leadership. Not so. Pretending doesn't require a platform. You can attend a weekly service, sing in worship, take up the offering, lead vacation Bible schools, or stay busy with all the usual church activities—and still not be born again. Emotional moments are not the same as spiritual rebirth. And surface-level religion is not the same as saving faith.

What are the marks of a pretender? Certainly, there are more than these, but let's examine five marks of a pretender.

Five Marks of a Pretender:

1. They Wear the Name of Jesus but Refuse His Commands: They might quote Scripture, lead worship, or raise their hands during service. However, they choose self over surrender with daily obedience. They live in disobedience and use Christian language to cover it up. Jesus said:

> *"Why do you call me 'Lord, Lord,' and not do what I tell you?" (Luke 6:46)*

2. They Confuse Emotion for Surrender: Like rocky soil, they receive the gospel with joy and enthusiasm, but fall away when trials come. They mistake Holy Ghost bumps for grace. Their faith is rooted in feelings, **not in Christ**.

"As for what was sown on rocky ground, this is the one who hears the word and immediately receives it with joy, yet has no root in himself, but endures for a while, and when tribulation or persecution arises on account of the word, immediately he falls away."
(Matthew 13:20-21)

3. They Love the World More Than They Love Jesus: They want the peace of Jesus but not the pain of the cross—Heaven without holiness. Their loyalty lies with comfort, culture, and convenience, not Christ. Paul dealt with the same issue in his day.

"For Demas, in love with this present world, has deserted me..." (2 Timothy 4:10)

4. They Clean the Outside but Avoid Heart Change: They attend church, get baptized, and behave well, but that's not salvation. Obedience and fruit are the evidence of salvation. Look at what Jesus said to the religious people of His day:

"For you are like whitewashed tombs, which outwardly appear beautiful, but within are full of dead people's bones and all uncleanness."
(Matthew 23:27)

5. Eventually, They Walk Away: Pretending has a shelf life. Eventually, the mask cracks. The fruit—or the lack of it—shows. They drift—not because they *lost* their salvation, but because they never had it. Sometimes, the difference between pretending and contending isn't dramatic; it's subtle.

"They went out from us, but they were not of us..."
(1 John 2:19)

Mini Parable. Two Worshipers.

Two men walk into the same church. One lifts his hands during worship. The other takes notes during the sermon. Both appear engaged and passionate. Yet, only one obeys Jesus on Monday. The other forgets the message by lunchtime. There is no conviction, no repentance—just a fleeting moment of inspiration with no lasting transformation. What was the difference between these two men? One was changed; the other was simply entertained.

The Marks of a Contender: What True Faith Looks Like

Paul never described Christianity as passive. He called it a race, a fight, and a battle. Because faith that saves is faith that moves, it's a faith that fights the good fight. It's a faith that endures. A contender isn't perfect, but they are pursuing. They don't coast—they contend. These five traits reveal the truth:

1. They Surrender Fully to Jesus: They don't just believe in Jesus—they follow Him, even when it's costly, unpopular, or painful. They do not negotiate with obedience.

"If anyone would come after me, let him deny himself and take up his cross daily and follow me." (Luke 9:23)

2. They Crave God's Voice Through His Word: True believers feast on God's Word. They don't just read it; they allow it to read them. There's hunger, growth, and transformation.

"Like newborn infants, long for the pure spiritual milk, that by it you may grow up into salvation." (1 Peter 2:2)

3. They Bear Lasting Fruit: Real faith produces real change. The fruit of the Spirit—love, joy, peace, patience, kindness, goodness, faithfulness, gentleness, and self-control—is not optional; it's the evidence.

"You will recognize them by their fruits."(Matthew 7:16)

4. They Persevere Under Pressure: Trials don't crush contenders; they refine them. Storms don't sink them; they strengthen them. Hardship doesn't prove their faith is weak; it proves it's real.

"Count it all joy... when you meet trials... the testing of your faith produces steadfastness." (James 1:2-3)

5. They Are Led by the Holy Spirit: Contenders don't just attend church; they walk with God. They fall, but they rise, repent, and keep running. They're not chasing perfection; they're chasing Jesus.

"My sheep hear my voice, and I know them, and they follow me." (John 10:27)

Real Story: 50 Years of Pretending

In our church, there's a precious woman we all call Nana. Her name is Linda, and she's 75 years old. Just a few months ago, she had a revelation and was born again, not re-dedicated, not recommitting to a faith she once had. She realized she had never been truly saved. Not "getting serious" this time. **Born again!**

At age 25, she prayed the prayer, got baptized, and joined a church. On the outside, it looked legitimate. But on the inside? "I knew I wasn't born again," she told us.

"I had too much pride to admit it. I was ashamed. Embarrassed. I didn't want anyone to know." So, for 50 years, she pretended. She showed up, served, and smiled with her Bible in hand. But at night, she lay awake wondering: What if I'm not really saved?

Until one day, grace broke through. She surrendered, repented, and believed. Everything changed. Her pride crumbled. Her hunger for the Word ignited. Her prayers became personal, not scripted. Her heart softened. Her joy became contagious.

Now, she worships with tears and joy in her voice because she knows what it feels like to finally be free. And if God can save Linda after 50 years of pretending, He can save you, too.

Eternity is Too Long to Be Wrong

"There is a way that seems right to a man, but its end is the way to death." (Proverbs 14:12)

There's nothing more dangerous than being convinced you're saved when you're not. Paul didn't tell unbelievers to examine themselves; he told the church. Why? Because self-deception is real, and eternity is too long to be wrong.

You can deceive others. You can even deceive yourself. But you can't deceive God. He sees the heart. He weighs the motives. He tests the fruit.

"Do not be deceived: God is not mocked, for whatever one sows, that will he also reap. For the one who sows to his own flesh will from the flesh reap corruption, but the one who sows to the Spirit will from the Spirit reap eternal life." (Galatians 6:7-8)

Jesus said many will expect to hear: "Well done, good and faithful servant." But instead, they'll hear:

"I never knew you; depart from me..." (Matthew 7:23)

Don't gamble with your eternity. Make sure. Follow the One worth following. Jesus isn't returning for casual churchgoers. He's coming for a fully surrendered Bride—burning with devotion and not lukewarm in belief. Jesus laid down His life for you. He wore your shame. He endured the cross. He conquered the grave.

Jesus didn't do these things so that you could settle for religion—He did them so that you could know Him. Jesus is not calling you to a checklist. He's calling you to the cross. He's not asking you to perform. He's asking for your whole life.

Final Challenge. Which One Are You?

This is your moment. Your mirror moment. Not to be right—but to be real. Not to check a box, quote a verse, or quiet your doubts. But to ask the questions that echo into eternity:

- Am I a contender... or a pretender?
- Have I truly surrendered, or am I just performing?
- Do I follow Jesus daily, or simply claim to believe?
- Is my faith bearing fruit, or is it just producing religious activity?

Take 15 minutes today without distractions: no phone, no playlist, no noise. Just you, your Bible, and the Holy Spirit. Read Psalm 139:23-24. Let those words penetrate beyond your surface. Ask God to search your heart, and when He speaks... respond.

This is where you lay down your pride, drop the excuses, and tear up the script. Don't leave that moment without making things right with God. Don't gamble with your eternity. Because when the fire comes—and it will—pretenders crumble.

This isn't a call to try harder. This is a call to die deeper. To lose the mask. To lose yourself, and to finally find the only One worth following. Eternity is too long to be wrong. So, get real, get right, and get in the race.

When the church conforms to culture, it ceases to be the Church.

CHAPTER 7

Awaken to Wokeism
How the Culture War is a Spiritual War

"Woe to those who call evil good and good evil, who put darkness for light and light for darkness..."
(Isaiah 5:20)

The Boiling Frog: How the Culture Shifted Without Us Noticing

I remember sitting in a coffee shop, scrolling through headlines. A Christian teacher was fired for reading Scripture aloud. A college student loses a scholarship for believing the Bible. A drag show was hosted at a public library... for children.

That's when it hit me:

The culture isn't shifting slowly anymore—it's sprinting toward deception. And much of the Church? Still sitting in the pot.

That morning in the cafe reminded me of something my pawpaw once told me. I have always loved the outdoors, and I can't precisely pinpoint when my passion started, but hunting and fishing have played a huge part in my life. One of the most vivid pieces of advice I ever heard came from him, and it has stuck with me ever since.

> *"There's an old parable about a frog and a pot of water. Drop the frog into boiling water, and it'll leap out instantly. But put it in lukewarm water and slowly raise the heat, and the frog won't even realize it's being boiled alive."*

It may seem like just a fable, but it is one of the most accurate descriptions of what has happened in our culture. We didn't wake up one morning in a post-truth society. It happened gradually, degree by degree, decade by decade. The moral temperature was slowly raised until things that once shocked us now entertain us. What was once a sin is now celebrated. What was once holy is now mocked.

And perhaps most tragically, much of the Church stayed in the pot. We didn't leap out. We became comfortable. We grew quiet. We became compliant. Somewhere along the way, we forgot that following Jesus means standing out, not blending in.

We now live in a world where sin is rebranded as self-expression. Speaking the truth is labeled as hate speech. Conviction is called intolerance. And the gospel is being edited to be more "palatable."

Take a Look Around

A biological man is celebrated as brave for winning a women's competition. A teacher is fired for quoting Scripture. A believer loses a scholarship for not affirming what the Bible calls sin. We've gone from **"live and let live" to "celebrate or be canceled."**

But let's be clear: cultural decline isn't just a social issue; it's a spiritual one. This isn't merely political unrest—it's prophetic. The Church must wake up. This is a war for souls. Wokeism is the elevation of self above truth, feelings above facts, and identity above God.

What Is Wokeism... Really?

Before we confront it, we need to understand it. The term "woke" started as a call to awareness about racial and social injustice. In its original form, it wasn't entirely wrong. However, like many movements, it didn't stay where it started. It evolved—mutated—into something else entirely. What began as sensitivity morphed into supremacy. Today, wokeism isn't just a buzzword—it's a belief system. A religion without a god. It preaches tolerance but practices censorship. It's filled with dogma and devoid of grace.

It redefines morality, cancels truth, and worships self. What God calls sin, the world calls progress. Personal feelings now outweigh absolute truth. Identity, preference, and emotion have become the new trinity.

At its core, woke isn't just a cultural trend—it's rebellion disguised as virtue. It dethrones God and enthrones man. It's not just wrong—it's dangerous. And here's the deeper layer most people overlook:

Wokeism isn't the real enemy— it's the weapon.

The real enemy is the same serpent from Genesis chapter 3, whispering the same ancient lie: *"Did God really say?"*

The Culture War Is a Spiritual War

I don't understand why more people don't see it. The battle we're in—it's not political. It's not generational. It's not left vs. right. It's light vs. darkness. It's clarity vs.

confusion. It's the Kingdom of God vs. the Kingdom of Self.

"For our struggle is not against flesh and blood, but against the rulers, against the authorities, against the powers of this dark world..." (Ephesians 6:12 NIV)

This is a war for truth, a battle for minds, and a war for the hearts of all people. Satan doesn't need people to worship him; all he needs is for them to reject God.

Lucifer is subtle, strategic, and deadly effective. He doesn't need a pitchfork; he uses platforms. He doesn't need to burn churches; he just needs pulpits to fall silent. He doesn't need to tempt you with evil—only convince you that evil is good.

"The god of this age has blinded the minds of unbelievers..." (2 Corinthians 4:4 NIV)

This isn't about politics—it's about principalities.

If we don't start seeing the spiritual layer beneath the headlines, we'll continue trying to fix kingdom problems with earthly solutions.

If you're exhausted by the shouting and division, good. That means you still care. But don't confuse the noise with the real battle. The enemy isn't in Washington. The enemy isn't on social media. He's ancient, and he's after your soul. But this isn't just happening out there—it's crept into the pews and pulpits.

How Wokeism Has Infiltrated the Church

We've spent years warning that the danger lies outside the church walls. But let's be honest: it's not just outside anymore; it's also inside.

The pot is boiling. Instead of resisting the heat, many churches have lowered their conviction to maintain peace. At some point, somewhere, biblical authority was supplanted by personal feelings. Truth became negotiable. Scripture became optional. Sermons today sound more like TED Talks than prophetic truth. Why? Because in our churches today, offending people has become a greater fear than disobeying God. This led to a new gospel: social justice over biblical justice.

God commands us to seek justice, but not at the expense of righteousness. Justice without Jesus becomes idolatry; it's zeal without truth. Then came the next step: **prioritizing inclusivity over holiness.**

Yes, Jesus welcomes all. But he transforms everyone who comes. He didn't die to affirm us; He died to redeem us. Love without truth isn't love; it's deception wrapped in comfort. All of this leads to one inevitable result: the fear of man replacing the fear of God.

Today, some leaders fear cancellation more than conviction. The early Church faced imprisonment and death for speaking the truth, while many today won't risk a comment thread.

So, ask yourself:
- When did we stop calling sin what it is?
- When did comfort become more important than conviction?
- Are we still building churches… or platforms?

Because here's the sobering reality: *When the Church conforms to culture, it ceases to be the Church.* We were never called to echo the world. We were called to confront it with love, power, and truth.

What Does the Bible Say About This?

None of this should shock us. Scripture is painfully clear about the days in which we are living:

"For the time is coming when people will not endure sound teaching, but having itching ears they will accumulate for themselves teachers to suit their own passions." (2 Timothy 4:3)

"The Spirit clearly says that in later times some will abandon the faith and follow deceiving spirits and things taught by demons." (1 Timothy 4:1 NIV)

"Indeed, all who desire to live a godly life in Christ Jesus will be persecuted." (2 Timothy 3:12)

Jesus didn't sugarcoat it. The closer we get to His return, the more deception will spread—and the more courage it will take to stand.

How to Stand Firm

How can we avoid the boiling pot? How can we live as light in a culture that has gone dim? Here's how:

1. Be anchored in the Word.
Truth isn't fluid; it's firm. God's Word isn't just helpful—it's essential. A Bible that you never open won't protect you from lies.

"Sanctify them in the truth; your word is truth."
(John 17:17)
108

2. Speak truth with love and boldness.

Silence in the face of deception is not love—it's compromise. Truth may cost you popularity, but it will never cost you your soul.

> *"If the world hates you, keep in mind that it hated me first." (John 15:18 NIV)*

3. Refuse to compromise.

Daniel didn't eat Babylon's food or bow to its idols. He stood firm, and God backed him. We're not called to go along to get along; we're called to be set apart.

> *"But Daniel resolved not to defile himself..." (Daniel 1:8 NIV)*

4. Surround yourself with truth-tellers.

Lone wolves get picked off. Don't walk this path alone. Find people who sharpen your faith, not dull it. If you've stopped gathering and isolated yourself, you're likely already in the frying pan, and the heat is rising.

> *"Not giving up meeting together... but encouraging one another." (Hebrews 10:25 NIV)*

5. Pray for wisdom and discernment.

The Holy Spirit is not confused. He leads us into truth, so ask Him for eyes to see.

"But when he, the Spirit of truth, comes, he will guide you into all the truth." (John 16:13 NIV)

You might be thinking: *But does anyone live this way anymore?*

Modern Daniels: Stories from the Furnace

We don't need to look back to Bible times to find boldness. The furnace is still burning, and there are still men and women who refuse to bow.

Consider Coach Joe Kennedy, the high school football coach who was fired for praying on the field after games. He didn't yell at anyone. He didn't create a scene. He simply knelt in silent prayer—and lost his job. However, he stood firm. After a years-long battle, the Supreme Court ruled in his favor. He got his job back, not because he shouted louder than culture, but because he refused to back down in the face of it.

Or Riley Gaines, the female athlete who bravely spoke out after a biological male took her place on the podium. She didn't curse the darkness—she told the truth. For this, she was mocked, attacked, and labeled. Yet, she kept standing.

These aren't perfect people, but they are bold ones. They're proof that God still honors those who stand in the fire. He still backs those who stand for truth. And whether the platform is a football field or a podium, the question remains:

Will you stand—or bow?

The Cost of Truth

Here's the part we've sugarcoated for far too long: Standing up for the truth can be costly. You might lose followers, opportunities, comfort, and relationships. The Early Church knew this. They were beaten, stoned, exiled, and executed—not because they were unkind but because they were unshakably faithful.

Jesus never said the world would applaud our convictions; He said it would hate them. If your Christianity has never cost you anything, you might not be following the real Jesus.

"Blessed are those who are persecuted because of righteousness, for theirs is the kingdom of heaven." (Matthew 5:10 NIV)

The furnace is lit. The lines are drawn. And the next chapter of this battle will be written by your response.

Final Challenge: Will You Stand or Bow?

This is the fork in the road. We cannot walk both paths. We cannot bow to culture and stand for Christ at the same time. So, let's ask some honest questions.

- Are there places where I have compromised God's Word to avoid conflict?

- Has today's culture kept me silent when I should speak up?

- Am I more concerned with being liked... or with being faithful?

This isn't about being political. It's about being **prophetic**. It's about living **unashamed** of the gospel in a world that desperately needs it—even when that world doesn't want it. You will either conform to culture or be transformed by Christ. **There is no neutral ground**.

So take a deep breath, and ask the Holy Spirit:

- **Where have I bowed to culture?**
- **Where have I stayed silent?**
- **What needs to change today?**

This isn't just a call to awareness; it's a call to action.

- Resist the temptation to remain where you are.
- Repent for where you've strayed.
- Rise to the place you've been called.
- Refuse to bow to the pressures of this world.

Do it now—while there's still time!

"Choose this day whom you will serve." (Joshua 24:15)

Grace alone,

by faith alone,

doesn't just save you—

It compels you to follow.

CHAPTER 8

Grace Alone by Faith Alone to FOLLOW

"For it is by grace you have been saved, through faith—
and this is not from yourselves, it is the gift of God—
not by works, so that no one can boast."
(Ephesians 2:8–9 NIV)

When Grace Is Misunderstood

He went to youth group, got baptized, and even led worship in college. But now? He's living with his girlfriend, hasn't opened his Bible in years and if you ask him, "Are you saved?" he'll confidently say, "Of course. I prayed the prayer and got baptized when I was twelve."

That's cheap grace in real-time.

Cheap Grace vs. True Grace

Imagine a man drowning in the ocean. He's gasping for breath and flailing in panic. Suddenly, a rescue boat arrives, and the lifeguard throws him a life preserver. It lands right in front of him. But instead of grabbing it, the man shouts, "I believe in this life preserver!" And then he sinks beneath the waves without ever taking hold of it. He didn't drown because there wasn't a way for him to be saved; he drowned because he refused to respond.

That's what cheap grace looks like. It's saying you believe in the power of salvation—while refusing to take hold of the Savior. It sounds ridiculous, but that's how many people treat grace. They believe in it. They quote it. They sing about it. They post about it on Instagram. But they never respond to it with repentance, obedience, or a surrendered life.

They believe in grace—but they've never been transformed by it. Yes, we are saved by grace alone through faith alone. But True grace is never alone.

True grace always leads to following.

That kind of hollow grace leaves people drowning. But real grace? It pulls you out and teaches you how to live.

Grace that Trains, Not Just Covers

Biblical grace is far more than a theological safety net. It is not passive or powerless; it does not lower the standard of holiness—it empowers us to live it.

The book of Titus says, *"For the grace of God has appeared that offers salvation to all people. It teaches us to say "No" to ungodliness and worldly passions, and to live self-controlled, upright and godly lives in this present age." (Titus 2:11-12 NIV)*

Grace doesn't merely forgive sin; it trains us to abandon it. It doesn't just cover your past—it reshapes your future. That's the kind of grace the Bible talks about: not a passive pardon, but an active force that produces transformation. However, today, grace has been distorted.

I previously quoted Bonhoeffer's words about cheap grace, and they deserve to be echoed here:

"Cheap Grace is the preaching of forgiveness without requiring repentance, Baptism without church discipline, Communion without confession... Cheap Grace is Grace without discipleship, Grace without the cross, Grace without Jesus Christ, living and incarnate."

That kind of grace is still being preached today. It poisons the church and leads people to destruction. True grace doesn't leave you as you were. It breaks chains. It calls for surrender. It teaches us to say no to sin and live holy lives. (Titus 2:11-12)

True grace is always costly. Not because we pay for it, but because it costs Jesus everything and calls us to surrender everything in return.

But today, the message of grace has been watered down and rebranded to fit our comfort.

You'll hear things like:
- "God loves me no matter what, so obedience doesn't matter."
- "I prayed a prayer, so I'm saved, no matter how I live."

That's not grace. That's a presumption.

What Grace Is…and What It Isn't

Grace isn't a free pass; it's power—power to be transformed, power to leave sin, power to obey. True grace doesn't make sin safe; it makes holiness possible. However, the modern message of grace has been reduced to slogans:
- "God accepts me just as I am."
- "Jesus forgives me, so I'm fine."
- "I prayed the prayer, so I'm set."

Some believe that because they once prayed, their salvation is guaranteed—even if their lives continue to reflect the same rebellion from which they claim to have been saved. That's not grace. That's deception. If someone asserts they've received grace but their life has never changed, they haven't received the biblical grace that the Bible speaks of. They've received a cheap counterfeit.

Faith Without Following Isn't Faith At All

One of the great tragedies of our time is that we've divorced faith from obedience. We've preached that belief is enough. We've separated believing from following. But Jesus never did. He didn't approach the disciples, saying, "Believe in Me and keep doing your thing." He said, "Follow Me." He said it to fishermen who dropped their nets. He said it to tax collectors who left their wealth. He said it to sinners who walked away from their sins. John wrote:

"Whoever claims to live in him must live as Jesus did."
(1 John 2:6 NIV)

That's not about perfection—it's about direction. It's about a life that aligns with Jesus's. Faith that saves isn't just mental agreement. It's not head knowledge; it's heart surrender. It shows up in repentance, in obedience, and in the pursuit of Christ. Anything less isn't faith; it's merely familiarity with Jesus without surrender to Him. And familiarity won't save you.

Dead Faith vs. Living Faith

James was blunt when he said, *"Faith by itself, without any action, is dead."* Dead faith says, "I believe," but never moves. Dead faith talks about Jesus, but doesn't follow Him. Dead faith stays the same. It's a belief that doesn't save. James took it a step further: *"You believe that there is one God. Good! Even the demons believe that—and shudder."*

Demons believe in Jesus. They don't doubt His divinity. They fear His authority. Yet, they don't obey Him. So, what kind of faith do we have?

Living faith doesn't just speak—it moves.

- Noah's faith inspired him to build an ark during dry weather.
- Abraham's faith led him on a journey without a map.
- Peter's faith inspired him to leave the boat and walk on water.
- The disciples' faith compelled them to leave everything to follow Jesus.

Faith that saves will never leave you standing still.

It won't allow you to remain in rebellion or drift in apathy. It draws you closer. It stirs you deeper. It pushes you forward. If your faith hasn't prompted you to follow, it's not the kind of faith that saves.

If your faith hasn't redirected your life, it was never rooted in Christ. This kind of faith has always been the biblical standard, contrary to claims that Paul and James contradict each other.

Paul and James: Not Opposites, But Allies

Let's clear something up:

Grace and obedience are not enemies, nor were Paul and James. Some attempt to pit them against each other, as if Paul preached grace and James preached works. Paul said:

> *"For by grace you have been saved through faith... not your own doing." (Ephesians 2:8)*

James said, *"So also, faith by itself, if it does not have works, is dead." (James 2:17)*

Were they contradicting one another? Not at all. Paul and James were confronting different lies.

- **Paul was battling legalism—**

  The notion that one can achieve a relationship with God solely through religious performance is misleading.

- **James was battling easy believism—**

  The lie that you can be saved without evidence, without fruit, and without obedience.

Paul and James weren't enemies; they were teammates addressing two different distortions of the gospel. Together, they paint a complete picture: we are saved by faith alone, but the faith that saves is never alone. It always leads to action and follows Jesus.

Bonhoeffer captured this perfectly:

"When Christ calls a man, he bids him come and die."

The Cost of Following Jesus

Grace is free. Following Jesus comes at the cost of your old life. Jesus never sugarcoated the message. He did not hide the fine print.

*"Whoever does not carry their cross and follow
me cannot be my disciple." (Luke 14:27 NIV)*

The cross wasn't symbolic. It wasn't jewelry. It was a death sentence. It meant your pride was gone. Your sin... surrendered. Your plan... laid down.

Grace calls you to repentance—not simply feeling sorry, but a true turnaround. Grace calls you to transformation—not a better version of you, but a new creation. Grace calls you to obedience—not as a burden, but as evidence of love.

Jesus didn't tell the woman caught in adultery, *"I forgive you, carry on."*

He said, ***"Go now and leave your life of sin."***
(John 8:11 NIV)

Jesus didn't say, "If you love me, sing to me."

He said, ***"If you love me, keep my commands."***
(John 14:15 NIV)

Jesus didn't die to make fans. *He died to make followers.*

Distorted Versions of Grace

Grace, in today's contemporary Christian world, has undergone rebranding: soft, sentimental, and stripped of power. Yet Jesus never offered grace without truth. Today, we see cheap substitutes everywhere.

- **Hyper-Grace**: Repentance is optional. Sin is not a big deal.
- **No-Lordship Salvation**: Jesus as your Savior—but never as Lord.
- **Cultural Christianity**: Church attendance, good intentions, and vague beliefs substitute for true surrender.

They all talk about grace, yet deny its power. Jesus warned us this would happen:

"Many will say to me, 'Lord, Lord...' And I will declare, 'I never knew you...'"
(Matthew 7:22-23)

That's not a scare tactic; that's love speaking the truth. True grace always transforms. If your life does not change after receiving grace, you may have never received the real thing.

Why This Matters: Eternity Is at Stake

This isn't a theological debate. This is about eternity. Jesus said the road to life is narrow—and only a few find it.

That means many think they're saved when they aren't. Many claim grace but never follow Christ. Many believe in Jesus but never bow to Him. False grace says, "Just believe—and you're good." True grace says, "Believe—and follow."

This isn't about earning your salvation. It's about evidence that salvation has genuinely taken hold of your life. If grace hasn't led to obedience, it may not have led to salvation. Because when you truly believe, your life will show it. Let's stop playing games with grace. This isn't just theology—it's eternity.

Final Challenge: Are You Just Believing or Truly Following?

Let's be honest:

- Have you embraced a kind of grace that costs nothing and changes nothing?

- Or have you encountered the grace that calls you to follow?
- Are you relying on a memory from the past, or are you walking in surrender today?

Jesus never said, *"Believe in me and stay the same."*

He said, *"Follow me."*

Bonhoeffer said, *"Christianity without discipleship is always Christianity without Christ."*

So ask yourself: Did I receive cheap grace, false grace, or true grace?

It's time to stop settling for the counterfeit and take hold of the real thing—because grace alone, by faith alone, doesn't just save you; it compels you to follow.

CHAPTER 9

What If I'm Wrong?

Eternity is too long to be wrong.

The Ultimate Question–Eternity Is on the Line

Picture this: You're standing at a fork in the road. One path is packed—smooth, easy, full of likes, smiles, and Instagram-worthy moments. People are laughing, vibing, and posting things like, "We're all on a journey. You do you."

It feels right. It looks right. It's easy, popular, and full of people convinced they're heading the right way. The other path? It's narrow, rugged, and uncomfortable. You can hardly see anyone on it—no crowds, cameras, or celebration. Just grit, humility, and surrender. Then, a man steps into your view, eyes locked on yours—calm but commanding.

He points to the narrow road and says, "That one leads to life. The wide one? It ends in destruction." You pause. Everything in you wants to question it. Let's be honest—the broad road feels safe. Everyone's on it. But then the man says something that shatters the illusion:

"If I'm wrong, you've lost nothing. But if you're wrong… you've lost everything."

Let that settle. This isn't a trend. This isn't religion versus relationship. This is the weight of the gospel. This is the tension of truth described in *Proverbs 14:12:*

> *"There is a way that seems right to a man, but its end is the way to death."*

The Eternal Trade

Suppose I'm wrong—if following Jesus with radical obedience, denying myself, and clinging to Him aren't necessary—maybe I've missed out on a few temporary comforts. Perhaps I chose the hard road for nothing.

If easy-believism, cultural Christianity, and feel-good faith don't hold up before a holy God, then you're wrong. We're not just talking about a bad day; we're discussing an eternal separation and forever regret.

This isn't about winning arguments. It's not about being religious. It's about reality. Because in the end, every soul will stand before the One who made them. And in that moment, the only thing that will matter is: Did you take the narrow road that leads to life… or follow the crowd into destruction?

People will say, "You're making salvation too complicated. Jesus is full of grace." And they're right—He is. But He's also full of truth.

"...and we have seen his glory, glory as of the only Son from the Father, full of grace and truth." (John 1:14)

Grace without truth isn't grace at all—it's just a lie wrapped in sentiment. You can't separate the two. Jesus never did. So, let's ask the hard questions:

What if I'm wrong?

What if salvation really is as simple as repeating a prayer once with sincerity? What do I lose? Honestly, not much. I still lived fully surrendered. I still obeyed His Word. I still walked in repentance. The Holy Spirit still transformed me. And if, somehow, that wasn't necessary? Then I still lived for truth. But now flip it.

What if you're wrong?

What if salvation requires more than mental agreement? What if Jesus actually meant it when He said, "Follow me"? What if just believing isn't enough—unless it leads to surrender, repentance, and obedience? You could spend your whole life thinking you were saved—only to hear the most devastating words imaginable: "I never knew you." And it happens more than you think.

Modern Story: The Deacon Who Doubted

Here is another story about a man I met a few years ago at work. He was in his sixties—a respected deacon, faithful churchgoer, husband, and grandfather. He leaned in, eyes filled with tears, and said, "I've been in church my whole life. I've served, tithed, led prayers… but I don't think I've ever actually surrendered." He wasn't emotional because of guilt—he was broken by realization.

"I kept thinking about that verse: 'I never knew you.' And I realized I knew about Jesus, but I never followed Him." That night, he finally bowed his heart, not just his head. For the first time, he found the peace he had been faking for decades.

He wasn't some prodigal who walked away. He was active, respected, and spiritually busy—yet spiritually dead. That moment became his rescue because truth, not assumption, set him free.

You could go to church, lead worship, quote Scripture, and even post about your faith online. And still… miss Him. Because you trusted in a prayer but never really knew the Person. So ask yourself: Which risk is greater? Which loss is eternal?

Jesus saw this coming. He warned us—not just once, but repeatedly—that many would be shocked in the end.

Jesus Warned Us—Many Will Be Shocked

Jesus didn't leave this open to interpretation. He gave one of the most chilling warnings in Scripture:

"Many will say to me on that day, 'Lord, Lord, did we not prophesy in your name and in your name drive out demons and in your name perform many miracles?' Then I will tell them plainly, 'I never knew you. Away from me, you evildoers!'" (Matthew 7:22-23 NIV)

These weren't atheists. They weren't skeptics. They weren't enemies of the church. They were people who believed they belonged. People who engaged in spiritual practices. People who appeared genuine. People who were active in ministry. But Jesus never knew them—because they never truly surrendered.

Jesus didn't say a few would be deceived. He said many. Let that sink in—countless people sitting in churches today who are good moral people. Even leaders will be shocked on that day. The question is, will you be one of them?

What If You're Wrong?

Maybe you're thinking, "Well, I believe in Jesus. That should be enough." But let's go deeper—what do you mean by "believe"? Remember, James said, even the demons believe in Jesus (James 2:19).

Judas walked with Jesus, witnessed the miracles, and still betrayed Him. Crowds followed Him... until the message became difficult. Then they walked away (John 6:66).

It's not enough to walk beside Jesus, post scriptures, or sing the songs. The question isn't: Have you been around Him? The real question is: Have you given Him your whole life? Being near Jesus is not the same as being surrendered to Him. One leads to transformation. The other leads to tragedy.

Jesus never said, "Believe in me and keep doing you."

He said: *"Whoever wants to be my disciple must deny themselves and take up their cross daily and follow me." (Luke 9:23 NIV)*

That's not casual. That's costly.

A friend once told me about a guy he had discipled—he grew up in church, led worship, and even preached a few times. Everyone thought he was the real deal. But when his life hit rock bottom, he said something I'll never forget: "I knew about Jesus... I just never actually followed Him."

That moment broke him—and saved him. Because it pushed him from religion into a relationship. I'll ask again: What if you're wrong? What if salvation really does require repentance, endurance, and surrender? What happens if you haven't truly followed Jesus, but thought you had?

This isn't about fear. It's about truth. Fear manipulates; truth invites. It's okay to ask hard questions — but it's not okay to ignore the answers. Truth isn't afraid of your questions. But apathy? That's the real danger.

Eternity is too long to be wrong

The Eternal Gamble—Are You Betting Your Soul? Some shrug and say, "I'll figure it out later." But later isn't promised.

> *"Why, you do not even know what will happen tomorrow. What is your life? You are a mist that appears for a little while and then vanishes."*
> *(James 4:14 NIV)*

Let that hit:

Your life is a vapor. A moment. A blink.

Now imagine there's a 1% chance your plane will crash tomorrow. Would you still get on that flight? No way. You'd cancel it in a heartbeat, warn your friends, and never step foot on that runway. Because the risk wouldn't be worth it. So why are we so casual with our souls—when the stakes are infinitely higher? The Bible doesn't say, "Assume you're fine." It says,

"...make every effort to confirm your calling and election..." (2 Peter 1:10 NIV)

You don't guess when it's a matter of life or death—you ensure clarity. You examine it. You test it. You make absolutely certain because this isn't a game. It's forever.

The Simple—Yet Costly—Gospel

Some still push back and say, "You're making it too complicated." No, I'm not. Salvation isn't complicated; it's just costly.

The gospel is clear: **Believe in Jesus. Repent of your sins. Follow Him—fully.**

That's it. Simple, but not easy. Free, yet not cheap.

Following Jesus will cost you:

- Your comfort
- Your pride
- Your plans
- Your old life

This isn't a half-in, part-time kind of faith. It's all or nothing. Cross or comfort. Death to self or live on your own terms. Crown Him, Lord—or crown yourself. Jesus doesn't just invite us—He commands us.

Yes, Jesus says:

> *"Come to me, all you who are weary and burdened, and I will give you rest." (Matthew 11:28 NIV)*

That's the invitation. However, Jesus also says:

> *"...repent and believe in the gospel." (Mark 1:15)*

That's the command.

And here's the bottom line: Jesus offers salvation freely, but He demands everything. You don't get the rest without repentance. You don't get the invitation without surrendering to the command. You don't get a new life without letting go of the old one. This isn't about adding Jesus to your life—it's about giving Him your life.

The Final Question –Which Road Are You On?

Jesus made it clear—there are only two roads. One is wide, easy, and familiar: the road of cultural Christianity, the road of belief without obedience, and the road of emotion without transformation. But there's another road: narrow, costly, and rarely chosen.

"Enter through the narrow gate. For wide is the gate and broad is the road that leads to destruction, and many enter through it. But small is the gate and narrow the road that leads to life, and only a few find it." (Matthew 7:13-14 NIV)

Which road are you on?

Final Challenge—Don't Wait Until It's Too Late

If you're still reading, it's because the Holy Spirit is at work. This is your moment. Not tomorrow. Not "once I get things together." **Do it now.**

Are you genuinely following Jesus, or merely claiming to believe in Him? Have you truly surrendered, or did you just repeat a prayer and hope it was enough?

If you stood before Jesus today, would He know you? You don't have to wonder. You don't have to guess.

"I write these things to you who believe in the name of the Son of God, that you may know that you have eternal life." (1 John 5:13)

But understanding begins with surrender. Here's the question that echoes throughout eternity:

What if you're wrong? Will you risk forever on a maybe?

You don't need a polished prayer. You need a bowed heart. A surrendered life. A real decision. Because eternity isn't worth gambling. Not when Jesus already paid the price for your certainty. Don't just bet your life on a prayer—bow your life to a Savior.

A decision without discipleship is deception.

CHAPTER 10

No Turning Back:

This Is What It Means to Truly Follow Jesus

"Choose for yourselves this day whom you will serve..." (Joshua 24:15 NIV)

Not Just Saved from Hell—Saved for Him

L et's be clear: hell is real. Eternal Judgement is real. Jesus talked about it more than anyone else in Scripture—not to scare people into shallow decisions, but to awaken dead hearts to a deeper truth. But here is what we've missed: Jesus didn't die just to keep you out of hell. He died to bring you to Himself. He didn't offer His life so you could breathe easy when you die. He offered His life so you could walk with Him now—love Him now, follow Him now, be transformed by Him now.

The gospel is not just a get-out-of-hell-free-card. It's a call to behold the beauty of a Savior who stepped down from glory, wore your sin like a robe, and took your place on a cross—not just to spare you from wrath, but to give you His righteousness, His Spirit, His life. This isn't just about what you're running from; it's about who you're running to.

Avoiding hell is a weak foundation for lasting faith. But Jesus? Jesus is the cornerstone that never cracks. He is worthy of your surrender, even if there were no flames to flee—because He is the Lamb who was slain, the King who conquered death, the One who calls you by name. The real gospel doesn't just say "escape judgment." It says, "come and die to self…so you can truly live."

The early disciples didn't follow Jesus to avoid hell. They followed Him because they saw something in His eyes—truth, life, grace, glory. And once they had seen Him for who He was, there was no turning back. You aren't just saved from something; you are saved for something. And more than that—you are saved for Someone. His name is Jesus.

And here's the real dividing line: Are you coming to Christ because you're afraid of hell—or because you've seen the goodness of the One who took your place? One response is driven by fear, while the other is motivated by love. Fear might awaken you, but only love will keep you surrendered. The Bible says it's His kindness that leads us to repentance—not just the threat of judgment. (Romans 2:4) Until you treasure Jesus more than safety, you haven't truly surrendered.

This Is It—The Final Fork in the Road

So if you've truly seen Him, you know there is no going back. Not to dead religion. Not to cheap grace. Not to half-hearted faith. The cross demands everything, and Jesus is worth it. You've read the warnings. You've seen the difference between the wide road and the narrow one. You've faced the lies—and now you've heard the truth. But none of this matters if you don't respond.

Imagine this moment like standing at the edge of a canyon. The only way across is a narrow bridge. It looks tight, uncomfortable... but it's solid. Built by the Bridge Builder Himself. And He says,

"I am the way. Trust Me."

But the crowd behind you shouts, "You don't need the bridge. Trust your heart. Follow your truth." Now you're at a crossroads: Will you trust the Bridge Builder, or take a blind leap and hope it all works out? This book has led you to the edge, but only you can take the step.

Indecision *is* a decision—and it leads somewhere. Delayed obedience is still disobedience. Passivity isn't neutral—it's surrender to the wrong side. This isn't something you can put off. There is no middle ground. There is no "I'll think about it later." Later isn't promised.

"How long will you go limping between two different opinions? If the Lord is God, follow him..."
(1 Kings 18:21)

What You've Heard vs. What Jesus Actually Said

Maybe you were told that salvation was just about repeating a prayer. Perhaps you were sold a version of Jesus that offered comfort, not a cross. Heaven, but not holiness. A moment instead of a life. But let's be clear:

A decision without discipleship is deception.
A moment without surrender is empty.
Faith that doesn't lead to obedience isn't faith at all.

Jesus isn't seeking fans. He's seeking followers.

No More Excuses—This is Your Moment

Some will still say, "I'll deal with this later." But again, later isn't promised. Others say, "I believe in God.

That should be enough." But James 2:19 tells us even demons believe—and tremble. Still, others lean on a prayer they prayed years ago. But the real question is: Are you following Jesus today?

"Today, if you hear his voice, do not harden your hearts..." (Hebrews 3:15)

This moment right now—this is your window to respond. Don't wait. Don't delay. The narrow road is open, but you must take the first step.

The Narrow Road—Harder, Holier, Worth It

Jesus never promised that the narrow road would be easy; He only promised it would lead to life.

"Enter by the narrow gate. For the gate is wide and the way is easy that leads to destruction, and those who enter by it are many. For the gate is narrow and the way is hard that leads to life, and those who find it are few. (Matthew 7:13–14)

The wide road offers belief without surrender and comfort without change. Most people choose the wide road. But the narrow road? That's the road of the disciple. It's marked by repentance, sustained by grace.

It doesn't just rescue you from hell—it launches you into the life you were born to live. Not just eternal life—but abundant, Spirit-filled, purpose-driven life starting now.

What It Really Means to Follow Jesus

If you're ready to stop playing religious games and truly follow Jesus, here's what He said:

- **Repent and Believe:** *"...repent and believe in the gospel."* *(Mark 1:15)*

- **Follow Him Daily:** *"..let him deny himself and take up his cross daily and follow me."* *(Luke 9:23)*

- **Obey His Word:** *"If you love me, you will keep my commandments."* *(John 14:15)*

- **Endure to the End:** *"The one who stands firm to the end will be saved."* *(Matthew 24:13 NIV)*

Jesus never said, "Pray this prayer, and you're good." He said, "Follow me."

This Will Cost You–And It Will Be Worth It

Let's be honest—this is where people hesitate. Following Jesus may cost you everything: your pride, your comfort, your plans, your old life.

Whatever you give up for Him, He replaces it with something eternal.

"For whoever wants to save their life will lose it, but whoever loses their life for me will find it."
(Matthew 16:25 NIV)

But don't let this cost scare you—because what you gain far outweighs what you leave behind.

This is the moment of Surrender

This isn't about hype. It's not about feelings. It's about truth—and now is the moment to respond.

"Choose for yourselves this day whom you will serve..." (Joshua 24:15 NIV)

"If you confess with your mouth that Jesus is Lord and believe in your heart that God raised him from the dead, you will be saved." (Romans 10:9)

If you're ready to truly surrender, pray this:

Jesus, I surrender everything to You. I turn away from sin. I choose to follow You. I give You my life. Be my Lord. Be my everything. Amen.

What You Do After This Moment Matters

This isn't magic. It's not just a moment. Saying a prayer doesn't save you—following Jesus does.

If you truly meant it, you won't walk away unchanged. You'll align your life with His Word. You'll make the changes you've been avoiding. You'll walk out of sin, not into it. You'll pursue holiness, not hype. You'll follow Jesus, not feelings. This is how you know it was real. This isn't the end; this is the beginning.

Final Challenge—No Turning Back

The world will attempt to pull you back. Religion will try to numb you again. However, if you've truly surrendered, there is no turning back. There is an old hymn that I remember singing as a child, and I am reminded of it daily, which says:

"I have decided to follow Jesus... No turning back."

This is where the uncommon Christian life begins. Not in perfection, but in pursuit. The only thing that matters now is to finish strong.

"I have fought the good fight, I have finished the race, I have kept the faith." (2 Timothy 4:7)

You may have prayed before, but now you've chosen the Person. You've left the wide road, picked up your cross, and stepped onto the narrow path—the only path that not only leads to eternal life, but transforms your life here and now. This isn't about someday in heaven. This is about walking in purpose, power, and obedience today.

This is what David meant when he said, "Surely goodness and mercy shall follow me all the days of my life..." (Psalm 23:6). He wasn't just rescued from danger—the Shepherd's goodness captured him. That's the gospel's invitation: come, not just to escape hell, but to know the One who gave everything to bring you home.

You've prayed the prayer before. But now you know—it was never about the prayer. It was about the life that followed.

CHAPTER 11

Now Go—Don't Look Back

Let's be clear—this wasn't just a book to read. It was a line in the sand. If you've made it this far, you've wrestled. You've questioned. You've probably had moments when you had to stop, pray, process… and maybe repent.

Good. That's exactly what was meant to happen. But now comes the part that separates the readers from the remnant. Because you can't unknow the truth, you can't unsee what's been revealed. And you sure can't go back to business as usual.

You've prayed the prayer before. But now you know—it was never about the prayer. It was about the life that followed. So, what happens next? That's what this final chapter is all about.

The Fire Must Not Fade

Let me be honest. One of my biggest fears in writing this book is that someone would finish it, close the cover, and do… nothing. No surrender. No shift. No repentance. No urgency. They'd feel something, maybe even cry, perhaps say, "Wow, that was powerful," but then walk right back into the lukewarm life they've always known.

Don't let that be your story. You weren't merely invited to feel something; you were invited to follow Someone. Following Jesus isn't a one-time decision—it's a daily death and a daily resurrection.

It's waking up every morning and declaring, "Not my will, but Yours be done." The fire that started while you read these pages wasn't meant to be a spark; it was meant to be a wildfire that burns away the fake and ignites something real.

Live it Out: The Daily Path of a Disciple

Step One: Walk It Out

What do you do now? You live it. You walk as if Jesus is Lord because He is. You repent quickly, obey immediately, forgive radically, and pursue holiness as if your life depends on it—because it does.

You open your Bible and allow it to confront, correct, and comfort you. You engage with a community of believers that not only makes you feel good but also helps you become more like Christ.

You stop asking, "What can I get away with?" and start asking, "What brings God glory?" This becomes your blueprint: Faith. Repentance. Obedience. Holiness. Power. Perseverance. Perfection isn't necessary, but surrender is essential.

Step Two: Don't Walk Alone

You weren't meant to fight this battle in isolation. Jesus didn't save you so you could become a spiritual loner. He saved you to be part of a body—a Church that's alive, equipped, and filled with the Holy Spirit. So, find those who aren't playing games and are serious about their faith.

Surround yourself with people who are serious about Jesus. You need individuals who seek God, not comfort. You need voices in your life that uplift you, not just those who agree with your compromises. You need friends who ignite your passion, not those who help you suppress your convictions.

If you want to persevere, you need a community that is devoted to the cross. If you can't find them, become that person, and others will thrive around you.

Step Three: Wake the Others

You weren't just saved *from* something; you were saved *for* something. Go and make disciples. That's not merely a suggestion; it's the assignment.

Jesus didn't say, "Come listen to sermons." He said, "Go. Baptize. Teach. Make disciples." This world doesn't need more people who identify as Christians. It needs people who live like Christ—people who burn with truth, love boldly, speak clearly, and refuse to water down a gospel that saves.

There are people in your life who are banking their eternity on a prayer they said when they were seven. They show no fruit, no repentance, and have no intimacy with Jesus. Yet, they believe they're fine.

You've read this book; you know the truth. Don't stay silent. Tell your story. Share what God showed you. Open the Bible. Break the lie of easy-believism in your circles. Call the people you love out of the dark and into the light. That's what real love does.

It's Worth It

Yes, this road is narrow. Yes, it's costly. Yes, you'll lose friends, face pressure, and be misunderstood. But Jesus is worth it. He has already carried every cross you will ever have to bear. Every sacrifice you make, He has already given more than that. And with every step you take, He walks alongside you. So don't stop. Don't bow. Don't shrink back. Go all in. Go after Him. And don't you dare look back.

Final Words

This book was never about making you feel better; it was about calling you higher. Not to perform—but to follow. Not to pretend—but to repent. Not to be religious, but to be reborn. And I don't say that lightly. I know what it is like to live a religious life and still miss Jesus.

My Surrender Story.

I was 33 years old before I truly gave my life to Jesus. I had prayed the prayer at seven, scared into salvation by a well-meaning message about hell. From that point on, I learned how to play the church game.

I knew the language, could raise my hands, nod my head, and even quote Scripture. But I was lost; I hadn't surrendered or repented. I had religion, but not Jesus.

For years, I lived for myself. I chased success. I worked hard to make money to acquire everything I wanted in life. I sought comfort, recognition, and control—and I achieved much of it. Yet, it never satisfied me. The truth is, I was building a life that seemed good on the outside but lacked a solid foundation beneath it.

It wasn't until I was 33 that I finally stopped living for myself and surrendered, allowing Jesus to become not just my Savior, but my Lord. Since then, I've had to unlearn a thousand sincerely wrong lies—things I was taught, repeated, and built my identity on. But God has been patient with me, and I know He's been patient with you too.

That's why this book is so important to me. It's filled with the truth, and I wish someone had shaken me awake years earlier. I'm not perfect; I've made mistakes—and I still do. But I know who I belong to now. I know what matters most. I no longer live for money or status. I live for one thing: to one day hear Jesus say two words— "Well done."

Ultimately, that's all that will matter. You won't be able to take your house, car, career, or Instagram followers with you. It will be just you and Jesus, eye to eye. And the only way to hear those words— "Well done"—is by living the kind of life those words are reserved for.

- Repent where needed.
- Rise to where you've been called.

- Resist the temptation to remain.
- Refuse to bow.

Do it now—while there's still time.

Don't let this just be another book on your shelf—let it be the moment everything changed. Jesus is calling. Answer Him with your life.

Let's Walk This Out

If you have truly surrendered your life to Jesus, or if this book has disturbed your comfort and reignited your passion, don't leave this moment unfinished. You weren't merely moved; you were called. You didn't just read a book; you made a decision. Now, it's time to act on it.

Your First Moves as a Disciple of Jesus:

1. Tell someone.

Let someone in your life know what Jesus has just done in you. Don't remain silent; this is your first testimony.

2. Get a Bible—and read it.

Begin with the Book of John. Invite the Holy Spirit to teach, convict, and accompany you as you read.

3. Find a Bible-preaching church.

You need a spiritual family that teaches the whole Word of God, walks in the power and anointing of the Holy Spirit, and disciples you with love.

4. Get baptized.

It doesn't save you; however, it does mark you. This is your first public act of obedience.

5. Start growing.

We'll help. We'll provide resources, discipleship tools, and methods to establish a genuine, life-changing relationship with Jesus.

Now—Take One More Step:

Scan the QR code on the following page. It will direct you to a short video where I personally thank you, encourage you, and guide you through what comes next.

This is where the book ends and where your new life begins.

I'M ALL IN

This isn't a moment. It's a move.

You've read the truth. You've been wrecked by it. Now it's time to *respond*. This isn't about hype, feelings, or another emotional high. This is about **surrender**—real, full, and final. It's not about joining a crowd. It's about crossing a line.

Here's Your Challenge:

1. Say It Out Loud—Then Live It

Visit: **www.theuncommonchristian.com**
Let the world know: *You're not just a reader. You're a follower. A disciple. A surrendered life.*

2. Get Planted

Find a Bible-preaching, Spirit-filled, disciple-making church. Get discipled—and **go make disciples**.

3. Burn the Backup Plan

No turning back. No safety net. No compromise. Delete the distractions. Block the temptations. Cancel the counterfeit comfort.

You weren't just saved *from* something—you were saved *for* something.

4. Fan the Flame

Commit to 30 days of:
- Daily surrender
- Daily Scripture
- Daily prayer
- Daily boldness

This isn't hype. It's holy.

And if you lean in, the Holy Spirit will light a fire in you that no lie, no fear, and no culture can extinguish.

Sign Below. This Is Your Commitment.

Name: _____

Date: _____

This isn't a contract. This is your declaration.

A declaration that you belong to Jesus, and you're not going back.

ABOUT THE AUTHOR

Jon Ellis is the founder of The Refuge Ministries of West Georgia, Inc.—a Spirit-empowered movement that has been transforming lives for over 15 years. What began as a step of faith and a gathering of just twelve people has grown into a thriving ministry that reaches the hurting, disciples the hungry, and brings hope to the broken.

Whether it's meeting practical needs or engaging in spiritual battles, The Refuge Ministries stands on the front lines—offering help that's real and hope that lasts.

Jon is a bold preacher, trusted counselor, and relentless disciple-maker. Whether he's ministering in church pews, school hallways, prison cells, or counseling rooms, his message remains the same: Jesus still saves, still heals, and still sets people free.

He and his wife, Wanda, have been married for 30 years and are the proud parents of two sons. Together, they haven't just built a ministry—they've ignited a Spirit-filled movement of hope, healing, and transformation for the broken, the bound, and those the world too often forgets.